Out of the Shadows,
The Acts of [Paul and] Thecla

TOOLS AND TRANSLATIONS

The Westar Tools and Translations series provides critical tools and fresh new translations for research on canonical and non-canonical texts that survive from the earliest periods of the Christian tradition to the Middle Ages. These writings are crucial for determining the complex history of Christian origins. The translations are known as the Scholars Version. Each work, whether a translation or research aid, is accompanied by textual notes, translation notes, cross references, and an index. An extensive introduction also sets out the challenge a text or research aid addresses.

Out of the Shadows,
The Acts of [Paul and] Thecla

A New Translation and Commentary

*Bernard Brandon Scott
and Perry V. Kea*

CASCADE *Books* · Eugene, Oregon

OUT OF THE SHADOWS, THE ACTS OF [PAUL AND] THECLA
A New Translation and Commentary

Westar Tools and Translations

Cascade Books
An Imprint of Wipf and Stock Publishers
199 W. 8th Ave., Suite 3
Eugene, OR 97401

www.wipfandstock.com

PAPERBACK ISBN: 979-8-3852-1924-7
HARDCOVER ISBN: 979-8-3852-1925-4
EBOOK ISBN: 979-8-3852-1926-1

Cataloguing-in-Publication data:

Names: Scott, Bernard Brandon, 1941–, author. | Kea, Perry V., author.

Title: Out of the shadows, the Acts of [Paul and] Thecla : a new translation and commentary / Bernard Brandon Scott and Perry V. Kea.

Description: Eugene, OR: Cascade Books, 2024. | Westar Tools and Translations. | Includes bibliographical references and index.

Identifiers: ISBN 979-8-3852-1924-7 (paperback). | ISBN 979-8-3852-1925-4 (hardcover). | ISBN 979-8-3852-1926-1 (ebook).

Subjects: LCSH: Thecla, Saint. | Acts of Paul and Thecla—Commentaries. | Acts of Paul and Thecla—Criticism, interpretation, etc. } Apocryphal Acts.

Classification: BS2880 T33 S35 2024 (print). | BS2880 (ebook).

08/23/24

For Margaret Ellen Lee
&
Jana Ellen Kea
Thanks for
Support,
Care,
and
Love

Contents

Acknowledgments

Arthur Dewey lent his expert advice on the translation, helping it adhere to the same translation standards at the *Authentic Letters of Paul* and *The Complete Gospels*. Margaret Lee read the complete manuscript and offered many suggestions for improvement. Sandy Shapoval, Dean of Library, and her staff at the Phillips Theological Seminary Library eagerly and efficiently provided the resources needed.

PART ONE

All About Thecla

1

Out of the Shadows

The Acts of Paul and Thecla is one of the stranger stories to have survived from the early centuries of the Christian movements. It tells the story of a young virgin who falls in love with Paul's preaching on continence, renounces her engagement to a rich Roman, and faces two condemnations to death. It is clearly a legendary tale, a popular tale, that makes no pretension to be historical. She baptizes herself and preaches the good news. Her freedom is enticing and extraordinary in the world of Greco-Roman patriarchy. Although its traditional title is the Acts of Paul and Thecla, the Acts of Thecla is more appropriate, so minor is Paul in these stories.

The discovery of the Dead Sea Scrolls (1946) and the Coptic writings from Nag Hammadi (1945) ramped up popular and scholarly interest in documents from outside the New Testament. The Acts of Paul and Thecla was not among the new discoveries, but had been around, hiding out in the so-called "Apocrypha."[1] Volume 8 of the *Ante-Nicene Fathers* (1885) contained a translation under the heading of "Apocrypha."[2] Later a new translation appeared in James, *The Apocryphal New Testament* (1924).[3] Apocrypha has a connotation of negative, to-be-avoided, spurious. As feminist interpreters of the New Testament and early Christianity explored

1. Apocrypha in Greek means hidden or secret. It is a modern category. The first collection under this title was published by Johann Albert Fabricius, *Codex apocryhus Novi Testamenti* in 1703.

2. "The Acts of Paul and Thecla." 8:487–492.

3. In 2005 this venerable collection was revised, expanded, and retranslated by Elliot under the same title.

the hidden stories of women, Thecla's story has come out of the shadows of the Apocrypha.

The Acts of Paul and Thecla was very popular for many centuries and circulated separately from the Acts of Paul. The Apocrypha, a collection of writings not in the Canon, is a modern creation. The Acts of Paul and Thecla have been locked up all too long in these collections. It is time to liberate Thecla's story and see what it can tell us about life among the early Jesus groups.

This new translation does not present Thecla's story as part of a larger collection, but showcases it on its own, putting it center stage. The translation uses contemporary American English, while trying to keep the style and tone of the Greek in the English translation. Since this translation is intended for a student or interested reader, we have kept the scholarly apparatus to a minimum, but at the same time employing the best textual evidence from the ancient languages. Likewise in the commentary that accompanies the translation, the emphasis lies on what the reader needs to know to understand the narrative, not the history of the various scholarly debates.

"Thecla in Context" tackles questions like when was it written? Where? By whom? What is its literary form? How does it relate to other writings from the Jesus movements in the second century? Providing reasonable answers to these questions can be exacting and completely satisfying answers can be elusive. We have tried to provide a clear path through the intricacies. "Thecla in Context" is more extensively footnoted than the translation and commentary so the reader can follow up on questions and debates of interest.

2

Thecla in Context

In the mid-second century the communities of the Anointed who looked back to Paul as their founder engaged in a debate over the status and role of women in their life. On one side the author of the letters we know as 1 and 2 Timothy and Titus (the Pastorals) favored the patriarchal values of the Greco-Roman world, while on the other the Acts of Paul and Thecla supported a radical vision of continent women living in communities without the support or direction of men.

From the late second century until the ninth century, the story of Thecla was much more popular than the letters of Paul to his two young disciples. But when these letters were incorporated into the canon of the New Testament, their traditional patriarchal and negative view of the role of women exerted a great influence on the church's position. They also determined a view of Paul as negative towards women. The Acts of Paul and Thecla gradually disappeared, leaving but a faint trace. Thecla was removed from the list of Roman Catholic saints in the 1960s, but still remains among the saints of the Greek Orthodox church.

The adventures of the young virgin Thecla will bring a modern reader closer to the popular imagination of those involved in the communities of Jesus the Master than any other writing we possess from the period. Most of what survives are the writings of elites, but the Acts of Thecla exhibit popular, people's story telling. But to understand Thecla's tale we must untangle a web of problems. Where does this story come from? What type of writing is it? Is it a separate tale or part of a larger cycle of stories? What is its relation to the writings of the New Testament? Who wrote it? Some questions we can answer; for some we will give our best guess; but others will remain unsolved.

Date, First Attempt

Around 200 CE, the North African apologist and polemicist Tertullian disdainfully dismisses a writing about Paul and Thecla that supports the notion that females in the Jesus associations should be able to teach and baptize (see below "Presbyter"). For dating purposes, this is the first mention of the Acts of Paul and Thecla. Since the Acts of Paul and Thecla circulated in North Africa before 200 CE, it must be dated no later than 180–190 CE.

The received version of the Acts of Paul and Thecla is part of a larger work, the Acts of Paul. Several scholars have demonstrated that the Acts of Paul utilized the canonical Acts of the Apostles as a source.[1] Pervo dates canonical Acts to the early second century CE, around 115–120[2], and Westar's Acts Seminar concurred with that dating.[3] The Acts of Paul, therefore, was written after 120–130 CE. The Acts of Paul and Thecla, therefore, could have been written no later than that date.[4] This would date the Acts of Paul and Thecla between 125 and 190 at the latest. Thus, the best estimate for dating the Acts of Paul and Thecla is 140–180 CE or, to make it simple, mid-second century.

Provenance

The stories about Thecla certainly originated in Asia Minor (modern day western Turkey). All cities or towns mentioned in the Acts of Paul and Thecla—Iconium, Lystra, Antioch, Daphne, Myra, and Seleucia—were in south central Asia Minor. The main events of the story are set in Iconium and Antioch. Tertullian also located the origin of the story in the Roman province of Asia.

1. Pervo, *Acts of Paul*, 67, for full evidence.
2. Pervo, *Dating Acts*.
3. Smith, *Acts and Christian Beginnings*, 5–6.
4. See Barrier, *Acts of Paul and Thecla*, 23–24; McGinn, "The Acts of Thecla" 2:802–3, more cautiously concludes that Tertullian provides evidence that the Thecla story (as an oral tradition) was known by the beginning of the third century CE. Codex Claromontanus (fourth century) contains a text of the Acts of Paul that includes the Acts of Paul and Thecla, indicating that a written version of our text existed at least by this time.

By the fourth century, the city of Seleucia, to which Thecla retreats at the story's end (4.18), was the home of a shrine and active community dedicated to Thecla's honor. The Christian pilgrim Egeria visited the shrine around 384 CE and reports in her diary about cells for female and male monastics built around a church that housed a martyrium (tomb) for Thecla.

> So, when I had come [to the martyrium] in the name of God, prayer having been made at the martyrium as well as all the Acts of holy Thecla read, I gave endless thanks to Christ our God who was gracious enough to fulfill for me, unworthy and underserving, my desires in all things.[5]

Authorship

The Presbyter

In his report about the story of Thecla teaching and baptizing, Tertullian claims to know who the author was:

> But if the writings which wrongly go under Paul's name, claim Thecla's example as a license for women's teaching and baptizing, let them know that, in Asia, the presbyter who composed that writing, as if he were augmenting Paul's fame from his own store, after being convicted, and confessing that he had done it from love of Paul, was removed from his office. For how credible would it seem, that he who has not permitted a woman even to learn with over-boldness, should give a female the power of teaching and of baptizing! Let them be silent, he says, and at home consult their own husbands (citing 1 Cor 14:34–35).[6]

While the later tradition accepted Tertullian's claim that an Asian presbyter composed the Acts of Paul, his hostility toward this writing makes his claim suspect. Polemical writings commonly discredit a work by raising doubts about the author's character and/or the circumstances of its composition.[7] To address the question, we must inquire into the relationship of the Acts of Paul and Thecla to the larger Acts of Paul.

---

5. McGowan, *The Pilgrimage of Egeria*, 23,5, pp. 147–48.

6. *On Baptism* 17, *Ante-Nicene Fathers*, 3:677.

7. Bauer, *Orthodoxy and Heresy*, is the classic study of how this works.

Manuscript Evidence

The Acts of Paul contains stories of Paul's travels around the Mediterranean, culminating in his trip to Rome where he is martyred. It features the only account of Paul's martyrdom (chapter 14). It also includes a Third Letter to the Corinthians (chapter 10). The story of Thecla is now part of this larger work (chapters 3–4). The manuscript evidence shows clearly that the Acts of Paul and Thecla circulated independently as well.[8] In fact, the manuscript evidence for the Acts of Paul and Thecla is stronger than the mostly fragmentary evidence for the Acts of Paul.

The Acts of Paul and Thecla are attested in Greek, Coptic, Latin, Syriac, and Armenian.[9] Several of the manuscripts are early:

- Greek Papyrus Hamburg: fourth century

- The Greek Bodmer Papyrus X: third or fourth century

- The Michigan Papyrus 1317 (fragment) and Papyrus 3788 (fragment): late third to fourth century

- The Coptic Heidelburg Papyrus: fifth or sixth century

More than forty manuscripts in Greek and other languages attest to the Acts of Paul and Thecla.[10] Furthermore, the Acts of Paul and Thecla are complete. By contrast, complete manuscripts of the Acts of Paul are missing; some portions, such as chapters 1, 2, 7, and 8 are fragmentary.[11]

Tertullian (circa 200) and Origen (200–250) both refer to a work entitled the "Acts of Paul." Tertullian knows chapters 4 (Thecla) and 14 (Paul's Martyrdom). Origen knew at least chapters 3 (Thecla) and 13 (Voyage to Rome). But the pilgrim Egeria, in 384, says that her entourage read the "Acts of Holy Thecla" (*actus sanctae Teclae*).[12]

---

8. Two other portions of the Acts of Paul also circulated independently, the letter known as Third Corinthians and the Martyrdom of Paul.

9. For a full listing of the manuscripts, see Barrier, *The Acts of Paul and Thecla*, xiii–xv; Pervo, *Acts of Paul*, 59–60; Hennecke, *New Testament Apocrypha*, 2:216–18. For Arabic, see Davis, "An Arabic *Acts of Paul and Thecla*: Text and translation, with Introduction and Critical Commentary," 105–51.

10. Pervo, *Acts of Paul*, 59.

11. Pervo, *Acts of Paul*, 59 has a translation of these fragments.

12. McGowan, *Pilgrimage of Egeria*, 23.5.

The discoveries of the Greek Papyrus Hamburg (circa 400 CE) and the Coptic Papyrus Heidelburg (circa 500 CE) indicate that a unified text of the Acts of Paul including the Acts of Paul and Thecla existed by 400 CE.

The Options

How do we sort out this evidence? What are the possibilities?

1. A single author composed the entire Acts of Paul, including the Thecla narrative. The popularity of the Thecla story resulted in its being excerpted at a later time. This is Tertullian's position.

2. The entire Acts of Paul was written by a community of ascetic widows who were receiving support from the institutional church.[13]

3. Stories about Thecla originated as oral legends in circles of continent women. The stories subsequently were incorporated into the Acts of Paul.[14] Afterwards, the two stories (chapters three and four) were excerpted to form the Acts of Paul and Thecla and circulated widely as an independent composition.

Independence of the *Acts of Paul and Thecla*

The manuscript evidence indicates a fluid situation. The fragmentary character of manuscript evidence for much of the Acts of Paul does not allow a definitive assessment of its literary unity.[15] The fact that the Acts of Paul and Thecla, 3 Corinthians, and the Martyrdom of Paul have a manuscript existence separate from the Acts of Paul suggests that it did not have a strong unified structure. In our judgment, the best explanation for this evidence

---

13. Davies, *The Revolt of the Widows*.

14. MacDonald, *The Legend*. With modifications this view is favored by Barrier, *The Acts of Paul and Thecla*. He thinks that Tertullian is essentially correct that an Asian presbyter wrote the Acts of Paul, but he argues that a female community produced the Acts of Paul and Thecla. Then the account was eventually edited by the Asian presbyter and incorporated into the Acts of Paul (22). Pervo, *The Acts of Paul*, 69, proposes an oral legend about Thecla, the current chapter 4, which the author of the *Acts of Paul* edited, and on the basis of which then composed chapter 3 as a preface to chapter 4, thus making Thecla into Paul's disciple.

15. A major problem for Pervo's proposal.

is that the author of the Acts of Paul assembled a composition from pre-existing elements in the tradition.

Several arguments support this hypothesis. First, whoever wrote 3 Corinthians had a good understanding of the Pauline letter form, something not otherwise attested in the Acts of Paul. The Paul of the Acts of Paul and Thecla bears little resemblance to the Paul of the authentic Pauline letters.[16]

Next, as Kraemer has argued, the gender perspective in Thecla's story heavily favors the female.[17] Although Thecla's mother Theocleia calls for her daughter's execution, the other women in the story support Thecla. Thecla is presented as an independent, brave, faithful, and resilient female. For example, Thecla's resolve to cut her hair would have been understood by an ancient audience as a break with her aristocratic values.[18] A woman's hair symbolized her marital status and her subordination to males.[19] Kraemer notes that Paul's command to Thecla to "go and preach God's word" (4.16) has no equivalent in the rest of the Acts of Paul (or the other apocryphal Acts for that matter).[20] No female characters in the rest of the Acts of Paul cut as large of a figure as Thecla. While Kraemer does not apply this evidence to the question of the independence of the Acts of Paul and Thecla, her insights reinforce the position that the Thecla story stands in tension with the larger Acts of Paul, implying its independence.

According to our thesis, the steps in this process are three.

1. The stories of Thecla emerged from and circulated orally in Jesus communities in Asia Minor, among house churches and continent women who challenged the traditional domestic and patriarchal values of Greco-Roman society. The character of Thecla suggests that these communities celebrated continent women who were itinerant, preached, possibly baptized others, and exemplified the Greco-Roman virtue of reverent piety (*eusebeia*). As such, the figure of Thecla was drawn in sharp contrast to elite pagan males, such as Thamyris and Alexander.

16. The Pastorals also exhibit little knowledge of the Paul of the authentic letters.

17. "Thecla of Iconium," 117–20.

18. "Thecla of Iconium," 137.

19. 1 Corinthians 11:4–5 indicates the importance of covering the head as an indication of female subordination. This passage is probably an interpolation into the original letter. See Dewey, *The Authentic Letters*, 110–11.

20. Kraemer, "Thecla of Iconium," 146.

2. About 150 CE, these stories were incorporated, along with other elements from the tradition, into a new composition: the Acts of Paul. In the evocative metaphor of Claude Lévi-Strauss, the author is a *bricoleur*, a collector and assembler of the traditions about Paul.[21] In order to fit the Thecla stories into the Acts of Paul and Thecla, the author/editor introduced Hermas and Hermogenes, the characters borrowed from the Pastorals.[22]

3. Sometime after 150 CE, the two Thecla stories began circulating separately from the Acts of Paul as the Acts of Paul and Thecla. As a separate composition, the Acts of Paul and Thecla was more popular than the Acts of Paul.

This hypothetical redactional history of the Acts of Paul and Thecla best accounts for the data. But the reader should remember that this hypothesis is not necessary to understand the Acts of Paul and Thecla. It can help explain problems, puzzles, and mystifications in the composition. But whether the Acts of Paul and Thecla had an independent existence in the oral tradition, as we and many scholars think, or was composed by a presbyter in Asia Minor, as Tertullian argued, it had a life of its own as an independent document for centuries. At best, it fits loosely in the Acts of Paul and makes sense on its own.

Pastoral Letters

In modern times 1 and 2 Timothy and Titus have been referred to collectively as the Pastoral Letters or the Pastorals because of their pastoral tone.[23] Although they claim Paul as their author, modern critical scholarship regards the letters as pseudonymous—they were written by someone other than Paul, but in his name.[24] Their vocabulary and style deviate significantly from the authentic letters of Paul. The Pastorals also make references

21. Lévi-Strauss, *The Savage Mind*, 16–23.

22. Those who see a connection to the Pastorals find their evidence in the editorial process. Dulk, "I Permit No Woman," argues for a strong dependence of the Acts of Paul on 2 Timothy, which he sees as significantly different from the other Pastoral Letters.

23. These letters were only called the Pastorals in the eighteenth century, after Calvin and Zwingli referred to Protestant clergy as pastors to distinguish them from Catholic priests.

24. Dibelius and Conzelmann, *The Pastoral Epistles*, 1–5, have a thorough discussion of this issue.

to organized church offices—bishop, elder (*presbyteros*), and deacon—that did not exist in that form in Paul's day. The eschatological urgency of Paul's authentic letters (e.g., Romans 13:11–12) is not present in the Pastorals. Although it is commonly assumed that the Pastorals know the Pauline collection, the actual evidence is slight. Like most second-century writings that refer to Paul, they understand him as a church founder,[25] not a theologian. The Pastorals are a fiction. They imagine Paul instructing his young students. As such, these are the only letters attributed to Paul that are addressed to an individual.[26] The Pastorals are not three separate letters, but a unified composition of three letters meant to be read together.

Dating New Testament writings is a quagmire. Traditional assumptions about authorship have resulted in inappropriately early dates. When Paul was understood to be the author of the Pastorals, they were dated to the end of his life, sometime before 60 CE. But once they are no longer understood to come from Paul's hand, more possibilities arise. But scholarship is conservative, often dating the Pastorals at the end of the first century CE.[27] When the Pastorals are examined independently of the authorship question, it becomes clear that their themes are at home in the second century CE. Their view of church order and understanding of Paul as a church founder fit well in the mid-second century. This dating is reinforced by dating the Acts of the Apostles circa 125 CE.[28]

The Pastorals envision structured, hierarchical church leadership based on the Greco-Roman household. Bishops (*episcopoi*, "managers") occupy the top tier of this community household structure (see 1 Timothy 3:1–7; Titus 1:7). They are to govern their community households as they do their actual households (1 Timothy 3:4), as a *pater familias* (head of household, i.e., the master). Timothy and Titus are the local heads of the household of God in their respective regions (see 1 Timothy 3:14–15). Likewise, elders (*presbyteroi*) manage local communities (see 1 Timothy 5:17; compare Titus 1:5 where "Paul" instructs Titus to install elders in every city). First Timothy identifies male and female deacons or servants

---

25. Vearncombe, *After Jesus*, ch 15.

26. Even the simple letter Philemon has multiple addresees.

27. Ehrman, *Brief Introduction*, 282, "near the end of the first century." Brown, *An Introduction*, 668, "the period between 80 and 100 as the most plausible context for their composition."

28. See above footnotes 5 and 6.

(*diakonoi*).[29] Female deacons are "to be sober, not slanderous, and temperate and reliable," whereas the male deacons "must not be married after a divorce [and] must direct their children and household excellently" (1 Timothy 3:11–12).[30] With the exception of the female deacons, the leadership is exclusively male. All such offices are missing in the Acts of Paul and Thecla.

The expectations of women are succinctly summarized in Titus 2:3:

> Likewise older women should have a demeanor appropriate for the devout, avoiding slanderous gossip and dependence upon alcohol. They should teach what is good. Their mission is to instill in young women the good sense to cherish their husbands and children, to be modest, pure, excellent homemakers, and subordinate to their husbands, so that God's message may not fall into disrepute.

Indeed, the Pastoral Letters parrot the conventional social roles assigned to women by the dominant Greco-Roman culture.

> As for women, I want them to appear modestly and moderately dressed, in appropriate outfits without elaborate hairdos, gold jewelry, pearls, or expensive clothes—none of that! The best fashion for women who profess piety is good deeds. Women are to learn in silence marked by utter submission. I do not permit a woman to teach or exercise authority over a man. I do permit them to be silent (1 Timothy 2:9–12).

To justify the subordinate and passive position of women, the author blames Eve, not Adam, for first sinning against God. "Additionally Adam did not take the bait, but woman did and thus sinned" (1 Timothy 2:14). The admonition concludes: "Women will, however, be rescued [saved] by childbearing, provided they persist in trust, affection, and holiness marked by modesty" (1 Timothy 2:15).[31]

---

29. *Episcopoi* and *diakonoi* are terms from the organization of associations, not households. While the household is the dominant model in the Pastorals, the group is clearly moving towards a more complex structure than the household.

30. All translations of the Pastorals are from Pervo, *The Pastorals and Polycarp*.

31. The view of the authentic Paul is very different. See Scott, *The Real Paul*, ch 11.

The Pastorals and Thecla

The character of Thecla could not be more out of step with the image of women in the Pastorals.

Acts of Paul and Thecla	Pastoral Letters
No church offices are mentioned.	Specific church offices are mentioned—bishop, elder, deacon (plus an order of widows).
Paul not called an apostle. Paul is a preacher and teacher.	Paul's apostolic status is emphasized (Titus 1:1; 1 Timothy 1:1; 2 Timothy 1:1; 2:11).
A household of females	Household headed by males
Thecla is authorized by Paul to teach the word of God.	Women are prohibited from teaching or exercising authority over men (1 Timothy 2:12).
Thecla is a young woman who has rejected the institution of marriage.	Prohibits placing women younger than 60 on the roll of widows. Expects younger widows to remarry, bear children, and manage their households (1 Timothy. 5:9, 11, 14). Women are expected to marry, raise children, and obey their husbands (Titus 2:3–5).
Sexual purity/chastity (continence) is a requirement for followers of the Anointed (3.5–6).	Continence is not required; church leaders are expected to govern their households well (1 Timothy 3:4; 3:12). The bishop should be the husband of one wife (1 Timothy 3:2).

The contrast between the Pastorals and the Acts of Paul and Thecla extends to their portrait of Paul. In the Pastorals, Paul is an apostle or envoy of the Anointed Jesus (Titus 1:1; 1 Timothy 1:1; 2 Timothy 1:1; 2:11). He is an older man near the end of his life (2 Timothy 4:6–8). He supports a hierarchical order for the community. Because the Pastorals were written decades after Paul's death, they draw upon Paul's status to legitimate the newly emerging offices of bishops, elders, and deacons.

As in the first generations of Jesus' followers, so in the Acts of Paul and Thecla, Paul is an itinerant, charismatic figure. His preaching inspires Thecla to reject her engagement and adopt a life of continence. While Paul is missing when Thecla is most threatened, he re-enters the story to authorize Thecla to teach the word of God (4.16).

The Pastorals and the Acts of Paul and Thecla not only represent different visions for the role of women in their communities, but they represent a profound clash within and among the communities that look to Paul as their founder. The Pastorals represent a version of life in the Anointed's household that seeks to live at peace with its pagan culture. Its leaders must be men with good reputations in the larger society (1 Timothy 3:7). These community leaders model the virtues of Greco-Roman society, especially as good managers of their own households (1 Timothy 3:2–4; compare Titus 1:7). The fictional Paul in the Pastorals urges Timothy and his community to pray for "monarchs and all of high rank" (1 Timothy 2:2) and "to submit to and obey officials and authority figures" (1 Timothy 3:1). The ideal women are married, bear children, and raise them according to the values of the dominant culture. They dress modestly and are subordinate to their husbands (1 Timothy 2:9–12). They perform good deeds (1 Timothy 2:10). For widowed women to receive financial support from the community, they had to demonstrate that they deserved this support because they have been married only once, done good works, raised children, and performed hospitality and service for believers (1 Timothy 5:9–10).

By contrast, in the Acts of Paul and Thecla Greco-Roman society is hostile to followers of Jesus. Powerful men in the story, Thamyris, Alexander, and the two governors, present a grave danger to Thecla. Had they proved successful, Thecla would have been killed. Even Paul, whose preaching so inspired Thecla, behaves inexcusably when Thecla is assaulted by Alexander.[32] Women's behavior contrasts with the Pastorals in another way. Thecla's mother, Theocleia, conspires with Thamyris, her designated husband to be, to end Thecla's fascination with Paul. When Thecla refuses, Theocleia calls on the governor to execute her own daughter. A second century audience can easily imagine Theocleia's motivation. With no mention of a father in Thecla's household, her engagement to the wealthy Thamyris would have provided the security that her mother Theocleia desired and needed. Thecla's stubborn rejection of the path expected of her by both her mother and society provokes Theocleia's call to "Burn the lawless one" (3.21). The mother represents the voice of a society that feels the threat to its patriarchal marital values by the gospel of chastity and continency embraced by Thecla. The young virgins and

32. Barrier, *The Acts of Paul and Thecla*, 9–10, argues that this is part of the plot of a romance, but here it appears to run counter to the narrative plot. Paul lacks insight into Thecla's call by God.

young men, when forced to deliver the kindling to burn Thecla, were reduced to powerless agents who must obey or face the punishment of their culture.

The depiction of the women in chapter 4 is particularly instructive.

- When the governor condemns Thecla to death by wild beasts, the women protest, calling the judgment "horrible" and "ungodly" (4.2).

- When the women of Antioch learn that Thecla has been charged as a "Temple Robber," again they protest this as "an ungodly decision" (4.3).

- As Thecla is brought into the arena for her ordeal, the crowd's response is mixed. Some call for the Temple Robber to face her punishment, while others again protest the judgment as evil. The women as part of the crowd are divided. Those who call for Thecla to face judgment are the only hostile group of women mentioned in the episode. Their voice represents the dominant culture and it reprises Theocleia's voice from the previous chapter. On the other hand, the women protesting Thecla's sentence represent the implied audience (4.7).

- When the lioness who protected Thecla in the arena dies, the women begin a sympathetic mourning (4.8).

- Upon throwing herself into the water, the "women and the whole crowd" yell for her to stop, obviously fearing that she will die (4.9).

- Most strikingly, the women come to Thecla's aid by throwing all manner of aromatics into the arena to throw the wild beasts off her scent (4.10).

- After the governor frees Thecla, the women burst into praise, "One is God who saved Thecla!" (4.13)

A major protector of Thecla is Tryphaena. She takes Thecla in as a surrogate or adopted daughter. She chases Alexander away (4.5) and stands between Thecla and the soldiers when they try to take her to the arena (4.6). When Thecla is released by the governor, Tryphaena transfers all her wealth to Thecla (4.14). Tryphaena is the ideal sympathetic and supportive benefactor and patron that communities of continent women desired.[33]

The depiction of Thecla is equally instructive. She rejects her engagement to Thamyris along with the life of domesticity it would entail. In the face of martyrdom, she displays courage, self-control, bold speech, and decisive action by throwing herself into the pit of water. As Kraemer notes,

---

33. Misset-Van de Weg, "A Wealthy Woman."

these are masculine virtues,[34] yet they characterize Thecla, not the elite males in the story.

The Pastoral Letters reinforce the traditional patriarchal values of the dominant Roman culture. Sober, self-controlled men rule their households and their communities, respecting external authority. Because of this, their bishop-leaders expect to enjoy good reputations among outsiders. Women and slaves know their place in the Pastorals' male-dominated social world.

By contrast, the norms and values of the Acts of Paul and Thecla collide with those of the Pastorals and the greater Greco-Roman social world. The elite males who should be paragons of traditional virtue clearly are the story's villains. By rejecting marriage and embracing the gospel of continence, Thecla sets out on a path where she exhibits socially recognized masculine virtues: bravery, decisive action, bold speech, and self-control.

Date, Once More

The sharp contrast in the views of Paul, church order, and the role women between the Pastorals and the Acts of Paul and Thecla has implications for the dating of the Acts of Paul and Thecla. As long as the fictional authorship by Paul controlled the dating of the Pastorals, they were dated earlier than the Acts of Paul and Thecla. But when the dating of the Pastorals is detached from the question of Pauline authorship, the issue of which one is prior can be reconsidered. Because the Pastorals portray Paul as a church founder who promotes a hierarchical church order and the subordination of women to the traditional roles assigned them by Greco-Roman patriarchy, a mid-second century date makes perfect sense. On the other hand, the church order of the Acts of Paul and Thecla is clearly the house church, the earliest form of community organization among Paul's communities. There are no bishops, elders, or deacons. There are no titles, period, except slave of the Anointed.[35] It shows no evidence of the organizational pattern from the association. Therefore, the stories about Thecla in the Acts of Paul and

34. Kraemer, "Thecla of Iconium," 147.

35. Demas and Hermogenes try to persuade Thamyris to denounce Thecla before the governor on the charge that she is a *christiana*, an adherent to the party of the Anointed (3.14, 16). But Thamyris ignores their advice. Thecla is charged with violating Iconian marriage laws. This could be evidence for the earlier composition of the Acts of Paul and Thecla and the later insertion of Demas and Hermogenes by the editor of the Acts of Paul.

Thecla represent an earlier period than the Pastorals. How much earlier? Who knows?

A Romance Novel

Recent scholarship has interpreted the composition of acts of various apostles as ancient novels, which became fashionable in the second and third centuries CE.[36] The canonical Acts of the Apostles is an early example of this novel type. The Acts of Paul and Thecla exhibits strong connections to the ancient romance novel.

Features of the Romance Novel	Acts of Paul and Thecla
Love stories focusing on the trials and tribulations of a young couple.	Pseudo-romance between Paul and Thecla.
The couple are separated by misfortune and struggle to stay alive and remain sexually pure (in the case of the woman).	Thamyris pursues his case before the governor. Alexander attacks Thecla.
The couple seek to reunite.	Each time Thecla is saved from death, she goes in search of Paul (3.23 and 4.15). She "yearns" for Paul.
The couple are assisted by divine interventions.	God sends a violent storm to rescue Thecla from burning. God strikes the pool of water, killing the seals that threaten Thecla.
Sexual and erotic overtones	Thecla kisses Paul's chains (3.18). She is stripped naked for the pyre (3.22) and the arena (4.8).
A contest in the arena	Thecla must face wild beasts in the arena (4.7, 4.13).
The couple successfully reunite.	The couple successfully reunite.

The Acts of Paul and Thecla exploits the novel's romantic conventions to promote a non-traditional role for women. Thecla desires Paul's teaching of sexual purity. Rather than affirming the female virtues espoused by the patriarchal structure of Roman society as the romance novels do, Thecla demonstrates manly virtues of decisive action, bravery in the face of death, and bold speech. She makes her woman's frock into a man's clothing (4:15), transforming a woman into a man! Earlier in the story (3.25) she cuts her

36. See the discussion in Pervo, *Acts of Paul*, 62–67; Barrier, *Acts of Paul and Thecla*, 7–10; and Calef, "Thecla 'Tried and True' and the Inversion of Romance," 163–85.

hair so she can travel with Paul. Kraemer points to this as her refusal to be subjected to males.[37] She does not become Paul's subservient spouse, but his genuine disciple and student (unlike the false Hermogenes and Demas). Paul commissions her to go forth and teach the word of God (4.16).

By using the tropes of the popular ancient romance novel to tell the story of Paul and Thecla, the Acts of Paul and Thecla gained traction with its audiences. At the same time, it presented a vision of life in the community of the Anointed that provided women options that deviated from the norms of an ancient society. Thecla's story entertained its audience and at the same time cleverly inverted the accepted patriarchal virtues.

Even though this romance is titled from antiquity the Acts of Paul and Thecla, Thecla is the main character. Paul hardly appears. Yet mentioning Paul in the title denotes the tradition to which this story belongs. It sees itself as part of the tradition which calls Paul its founder. Also, it presents Paul as the pseudo-romantic partner of Thecla. That dynamic makes the story work. Paul legitimates the story.

Whose Voice?

The Acts of Paul and Thecla shows us a narrative and social world where a heroine displays masculine virtues—decisive action, bravery in the face of death, bold speech, and self-control. Yet, for all her boldness, Thecla's modesty, a primary female virtue in Greco-Roman society, is always maintained and reinforced.[38] Likewise, the behaviors of elite men are revealed as violent and malicious. Thecla is a resistor. She rejects marriage to follow the message of continence preached by Paul. In so doing, she discovers a vocation and a voice, inspiring others as well. The audience for this tale was Jesus followers, probably women, attracted to the opportunity, community, and power Thecla represents. The story's romance form boosted its popularity.

The story of Thecla spoke meaningfully to communities of the Anointed on critical issues like martyrdom and continence. Its portrait of a brave woman willing to die for her convictions and a God ready to intervene to save her offered communities hope. The asceticism of The Acts of Paul and Thecla supported women who sought opportunities denied them by

37. Kraemer, "Thecla of Iconium," 137.

38. Hylen, *A Modest Apostle*, correctly accents the similarity in this regard between Acts of Paul and Thecla and 1 Timothy, but she overstates women's leadership roles in 1 Timothy.

the conventional social expectations for women—marriage, subordination, domesticity. But it did not reject marriage completely, nor did it explicitly advocate other forms of ascetic practice such as abstinence from meat and alcohol. There was something in this story for people who were at different points on the spectrum regarding ascetic practices.[39]

Whose voice are we hearing in Thecla's stories? We would like to think that it is the voice of women,[40] but is that so? There are some contradictions to reconcile. The main hero is a woman and the men come off badly. Even Paul has problematic aspects. The stories clearly appealed to women. The literary form of the novel was a popular genre and the Greek of the Acts of Paul and Thecla is the common koine Greek, not elevated, with few literary pretensions. Yet all the characters are wealthy, some in the extreme, e.g., Alexander and Tryphaena. Only Paul and Onesiphorus are poor. Perhaps the trials and tribulations of the wealthy make for a better story. Is the point of view male or female? While Thecla acts independently, dresses like a man, and becomes a preacher of the good news, her gaze is on Paul. Yet the male gaze persists as witness to notes about Thecla's beauty and nakedness. One should keep the ambiguity of voice in mind. Whose voice we are hearing remains unclear.

Who was reading the Acts of Paul and Thecla? Again, the consensus is that women were the primary readers.[41] Yet there are reasons to question that conclusion or assumption. Literacy rates were low in the ancient world, probably no more than ten percent in urban areas and always lower among women of all social classes.[42] Haines-Eitzen has turned a skeptical eye to this question. She examines twelve papyri from the pre-sixth century from the Apocryphal Acts (most of which are from the Acts of Paul) for evidence of who read them. She concludes: "there is nothing to suggest a gendered readership."[43] We should perhaps be cautious in too quickly proclaiming who was reading the Acts of Paul and Thecla. Its audience was probably

---

39. Barrier, "The Acts of Paul and Thecla: The Historiographical Context," surveys the various ways the *Acts of Paul and Thecla* has been understood.

40. Cardman, "Women, Ministry," 301, thinks it "offers a window to the world or early Christian women." This is a common position.

41. Davies, *The Cult*, 12–13. Tertullian also thought it was read by women, *On Baptism*, 17.

42. The classic study is Harris, *Ancient Literacy*. While often criticized, it has stood up well.

43. Hainz-Eitzen, *The Gendered Palimpsest*, 57.

mixed. Furthermore, it was intended to be read aloud, not silently. Its audience was surely mixed.

The Acts of Paul and Thecla is a romance novel, a fiction, and not simply a mirror into women's lives. Cooper has pointed out, "The Acts of Paul makes clear the usefulness of the heroine's continence as a narrative device to propel the conflict between the apostle and a symbolic representative of the ruling class of the cities he visits."[44] Thecla's continence represents a fundamental challenge to the Empire and its social values. Cooper perhaps states her argument too boldly when she argues that "it is essentially a conflict *between men* . . . not really about women."[45] But she makes an important point. Female continence is an important weapon in the contest with the Empire. The female body became the locus of contest not only with the Empire, but also within the Christian households as seen in the Pastorals. While the Pastorals is obviously a male argument about female behavior, the Acts of Paul and Thecla is not only an argument appealing to males competing for power but offers females an argument against patriarchy.

44. Cooper, *The Virgin and the Bride*, 54.
45. See the thoughtful critique by Osiek and MacDonald, *A Woman's Place*, 241.

3

Thecla Going Forward

Thecla and Ascetism

Beginning in the late second century, a new form of ascetism appeared among the Jesus groups that rejected marriage. Their critics called them "Encratites," from the Greek *engkrateia* meaning "self-control," and regarded their forms of ascetism as extreme. Hippolytus of Rome (around 170–235 CE) claimed that the Encratites abstained from animal food, drank only water, and forbade marriage.

> In respect, however, of their mode of life, they pass their days inflated with pride. They suppose that by meats they magnify themselves, while abstaining from animal food, (and) being water-drinkers, and forbidding to marry, and devoting themselves during the remainder of life to habits of ascetism.[1]

According to Hippolytus, the Encratites have three characteristics: rejection of marriage and sexual activity, abstinence from animal meat, and abstinence from alcoholic beverages. The author of 1 Timothy mentions two of these items when he warns about "liars" who ". . .forbid marriage and demand abstinence from foods, which God created to be received with thanksgiving . . ." (4:3).

---

1. See Hippolytus, *Refutation of All Heresies* VIII, xiii (*Ante-Nicene Fathers*, 5:124). Other references include Clement of Alexandria, *Paedagogus* II, ii, 33; *Stromata* I, xv; VII, xvii; Irenaeus, *Against All Heresies* I, xxviii.

The Acts of Paul and Thecla extol self-discipline (*egkrateia*: 3.5 and 8), and clearly value continence: "Congratulations to virgins whose bodies are very pleasing to God and will not lose the reward for their purity. For the Father's word will accomplish salvation in them on the day of his son, and they shall rest forever and ever" (3:6). Thecla spurns her engagement to Thamyris and vigorously defends herself against Alexander's sexual assault. But marriage is not condemned outright. One of the Congratulations does extol "those whose relations with their wives are as they were not."[2] But the faithful Onesiphorus is married and has children (3.2). The figure of Thecla certainly appealed to continent women. Married women could also enjoy her daring exploits and admire her faith and resilience without feeling that they must be continent like her. Her embrace of chastity imbues her with a charisma and authority that could be admired, but which need not be emulated by everyone.

Although the Acts of Paul and Thecla contain no explicit commandment regarding abstinence from meat and intoxicating liquids, the meal shared in the tomb by Onesiphorus' family, Paul, and Thecla consists simply of bread, vegetables, and water (3.25).[3]

The Acts of Paul and Thecla follows up on the historical Paul's position and foreshadows that of Encratites in the late second and third centuries. It stands between the two. Paul proclaims, "You are no longer Jew or Greek, no longer slave or freeborn, no longer 'male and female'" (Galatians 3:28). But Paul and his communities found it difficult to work out this new freedom, as can be seen in the Corinthians' questions to Paul: "Now about the matters you raised in your letter: I do think it is better for a man to abstain from sexual intercourse with a woman" (1 Corinthians 7:1). While Paul favors abstinence, he does not forbid marriage:

> Don't withhold yourselves from each other, except perhaps for a little while by mutual consent so that you may have the leisure you need to pray; then come together again so that Satan will find no opportunity to tempt you because of your lack of self-control. But I offer this advice as a concession, not as a command. I wish that everyone were like me in this regard; but we all have our own

2. See 1 Corinthians 7:29: "This is what I mean, friends: this period of opportunity <for our mission> is coming to an end. In what is left of it those who have wives should live as if they did not have them."

3. In 3.5 Onesiphorus serves Paul and his companions bread, which is a normal expectation.

special gift from God, one has a gift of this kind, another has a gift of that kind (1 Corinthians 7:5–7).

The Acts of Paul and Thecla moves beyond Paul by advocating continence and forming a community of the unmarried who practice continence, but it does not go as far as the Encratites in forbidding marriage. The Acts of Paul and Thecla are proto-Encratic. On the other hand, the Pastorals reject Paul's views in 1 Corinthians and foreshadow the emerging orthodoxy of the third and fourth centuries. These issues will entail a major ongoing debate within and between the communities of the anointed for the next several centuries.[4]

Martyrdom

Twice Thecla is nearly executed for her new convictions but is miraculously delivered from death on both occasions. Her deity intervenes to protect and rescue her. Other martyrdom accounts differ. In the Passion of Perpetua and Felicitas, set in the early third century, Perpetua is granted divine revelations to comfort and steel her resolve, but these visions make clear that she will die a martyr's death. Her story culminates in the account of her death. Thecla's story concludes with her deliverance in the arena and the formation of a new community or family of continent women.[5]

Ancient romance stories feature episodes in which a heroine faces a grisly death, only to be saved in miraculous and spectacular fashion. Unlike Perpetua's story, Thecla's narrative does not promote martyrdom. However, her resolve and bravery in adhering to her new convictions, even at the potential cost of her life, appealed to ancient audiences. Since martyrdom became a primary element in Christian identification and self-understanding, it was also highly debated.[6] Should martyrdom be sought out or avoided? How should communities deal with those who denied being among the followers of Jesus? While Thecla's story appealed to those who supported the ideal of martyrdom, it does not require seeking martyrdom. The tales of Thecla's miraculous deliverance from death offered a powerful,

---

4. Brown, *The Body*, ch 7, deals with the *Acts of Paul and Thecla*'s place in this ongoing debate.

5. Streete, "Buying the Stairway to Heaven," 186–205, for an excellent comparison of these two narratives.

6. Vearncombe, *After Jesus*, chap. 18. Perkins, *The Suffering Self*.

encouraging view.[7] Thecla's story became popular in part because it could be understood as supporting multiple views on the question of martyrdom.

Aftermath of Thecla's Story

Manuscripts

The continuing popularity of the Thecla story may be gauged in several ways. The Acts of Paul and Thecla circulated independently of the Acts of Paul and is much better attested in manuscript tradition (see above). The number of surviving Greek manuscripts and the different translations indicate that the Acts of Paul and Thecla was very popular and spread well beyond the Greek speaking areas of the Roman empire to other regions.[8]

Later Stories

Stories and legends about Thecla continued to expand, especially in ascetic circles. Around 300 CE Methodius, a bishop in Asia Minor, composed his *Banquet of the Ten Virgins*, a strongly pro-ascetic work. Thecla, chief of the virgins in this story, leads the final hymn in praise of virginity.[9] Although the *Banquet of the Ten Virgins* does not cite or refer to The Acts of Paul and Thecla, it does bear witness to Thecla's popularity in ascetic circles.

An anonymous work known as the *Physiologus*, a collection of beast tales dated about 300 CE, includes Thecla in a list of biblical figures who were saved by praying. She is included in a list of biblical figures who fled from evil; in Thecla's case, she fled from Thamyris. The *Physiologus* indicates that the Acts of Paul and Thecla was known to this author and that Thecla was considered a hero alongside other well-known biblical characters, such as Moses, Daniel, Esther, and Judith.[10]

Writing in the late fourth century CE, John Chrysostom refers approvingly to Thecla as an example of charitable giving.[11] Pseudo-Chrysostom's

---

7. Miraculous deliverance is also a theme in Jewish stories of the suffering innocent one—Daniel in the Lion's Den (Daniel 6), the Three Young Men in Fiery Furnace (Daniel 3:8–25), and Susanna and the Elders (Daniel 13).

8. See the essays in Barrier, "The Acts of Paul and Thecla."

9. Methodius, "Banquet of the Ten Virgins," Discourse 11. *Ante-Nicene Fathers*, Vol. vi.

10. Curley, *Physiologus*.

11. *Homilies*, 167 in Morris; see Pervo's bibliography (346) *Homilies*, 167 in

"Panegyric to Thecla" (fifth or sixth century) is a homily devoted to Thecla during the "Feast of St. Thecla, the Virgin Martyr" on September 23 in the West and the 24th in the East. The homily includes a story about how Thecla escaped sexual assault in the desert by becoming invisible.[12]

Isidore of Pelusium (431) referred to Thecla as "the first martyr."[13] Hence, she became known as the Protomartyr. Many of these writings treat Thecla as a martyr, even though there is no extant story of her martyrdom. That she twice faced martyrdom may be sufficient to count for the appellation. But in the third and fourth centuries the ascetics were the true successors of the martyrs. Their life of denial was understood as martyrdom. So, on both accounts Thecla is a protomartyr.

Shrine

By at least the mid-fourth century pilgrims were coming to Hagia Thekla, a shrine dedicated to Thecla, built on a hill outside Seluecia (modern Silifke, Turkey). In 384 CE, a Christian pilgrim named Egeria (see above) visited the site and recorded her visit. She reports that a shrine was connected to a church with monastic cells for men and women. Egeria reports that while visiting the shrine, she and those with her read "the Acts of Holy Thecla" (*Acta Sanctae Teclae*),[14] which appears to be what we call the Acts of Paul and Thecla.

The shrine's popularity demanded its expansion over time. In the second half of the fifth century, the shrine was relocated to a cave, and a small basilica was built into it. Around 476 CE, a larger new church was built (80 meters in length), probably under the patronage of the emperor Zeno. Construction continued into the sixth century with the addition of a public bath and several large cisterns. Davis interprets this as evidence for the "changing needs of a rapidly growing pilgrim clientele."[15]

11:329–564.

12. See MacDonald, "Pseudo-Chrysostom's Panegyric," 151–59.

13. Voicu, "Thecla in the Christian East," 60, for full references. See also Batle, "The Cult of the Female Proto-Martyr."

14. *Itinerary* 23:5. The entire account of her visit to Thecla's shrine is found in 22:2—23:6.

15. *The Cult of St. Thecla*, an excellent treatment of Hagia Thekla at Seleucia is in chapter 2.

Along with the continuing expansion of the shrine of Thecla in Seleucia, in the mid-fifth century an anonymous author (often referred to as Pseudo-Basil) produced *The Life and Miracles of St. Thecla*, an embellished and expanded version of the Thecla story. This writing is closely associated with the shrine in Seleucia. In the preface the author introduces Thecla as "the apostle and martyr." In the Acts of Paul and Thecla, Paul charges Thecla to go teach the word of God (4.16), but in *The Life and Miracles of St. Thecla* Paul adds, "and finish the gospel-spreading peace and share my eagerness on behalf of Christ. This is why Christ has chosen you through me: so that he might acquire you as an apostle, and so that he might entrust to you some of those cities which have not yet been catechized" (26).[16]

In the Acts of Paul and Thecla, after Thecla visits her mother in Iconium, the story comes to an abrupt ending: "And bearing witness to these things, she departed for Seleucia. Then after enlightening many by God's word, she fell asleep in a beautiful dream" (4.18). But the fifth century *The Life and Miracles of St. Thecla* expands on Thecla's work in Seleucia (*Life* 28). *The Life* claims that Thecla spent her days teaching and baptizing, "Having preached the good news of the saving word and catechized and sealed and enlisted many in Christ's army" (*Life* 28). The anonymous author portrays Thecla as a female apostle on a par with Paul.

At the conclusion of *The Life*, the author provides an etiology (origin story) for the Seleucia shrine.

> She by no means died, . . . but she sunk down while still living and went down into the earth as it was pleasing to God to separate and split open for her that ground in the place where the divine and holy and liturgical table was fixed, set up in a round colonnade shining with silver; and for every suffering and every illness she send forth streams of cures from that very spot, as if from some fountain of virginal grace pouring out cures from there for those who ask and beg. As a result it is a place of healing for all people, and is established as a common site of propitiation for all the earth. (*Life* 28)

The miracles portion of this work contains numerous accounts of miracles performed posthumously by Thecla. While *The Life and Miracles of St. Thecla*

---

16. Translation by Jacobs, *Life of St. Thecla*. See also the excellent study Johnson, *The Life and Miracles*.

did not enjoy the popularity of the earlier Acts of Paul and Thecla, it does underscore the ongoing importance of Thecla's cult at Seleucia.[17]

In addition to the above, alternative traditions have Thecla traveling to Syria and Rome. The cave of Thecla in Maaloula, Syria, seems to have been a pilgrimage site since the fourth or fifth century. The Catacomb of Thecla in Rome dates as far back as the late fourth century. These and other shrines to Thecla attest to the geographical spread of her cult.

Conclusion

Even though the Acts of Paul and Thecla did not make it into the canon, it offers a view of popular piety in the second century and an alternative view to that put forward by the Pastorals. It shows the heritage of Paul was still being hotly contested in the mid-second century. It raises an interesting question—if the Acts of Paul and Thecla had made it into the canon, how would the later tradition have understood Paul? The Pastorals led to a patriarchal view of Paul and editing of his original letters to bring them into compliance with the worldview of the Pastorals. First Corinthians 14:34 is a good example: "women should be silent during the meetings. They are not permitted to speak, but must be subordinate, just as scripture says. Women be silent."[18] This was inserted into a discussion of prophecy, interrupting the flow of the argument. This editing of Paul's letters in the mid-second century obscured Paul's real and radical views on the role of women.[19]

The canon of the New Testament is a product of the fourth and fifth centuries. Its formation was not inevitable and how it came to be is largely unknown. Compared to the Pastorals, the Acts of Paul and Thecla have at least as strong, if not a stronger case to follow in the authentic tradition of Paul. Canonicity is a theological judgment, not a historical one.

The Acts of Paul and Thecla or The Acts of Holy Thecla, as the pilgrim Egeria has it, offers not only a chance to see the debates in the second century in an entirely new way. It also shows Paul in a new light and asks, was it all inevitable? Could the history of Christianity have developed differently? Thecla answers, "Yes!"

---

17. Davis, *The Cult of St. Thecla*, ch. 4, "Pilgrimage and the Cult of St. Thecla in the Mareotis."

18. Dewey, *The Authentic Letters of Paul*, 112.

19. Scott, *The Real Paul*, chap. 11.

Map of Roman Asia

From *Atlas of the Historical Geography of the Holy Land,* by George Adam Smith (1915). This image is in the public domain. Wikimedia Commons: https://commons. wikimedia.org/wiki/File:Asia_Minor_showing_positions_of_the_Seven_Churches_ (Smith,_1915).jpg/.

Seven cities are mentioned in the Acts of Paul and Thecla, all located in Roman Asia.

1. Iconium

2. Lystra

3. Antioch in Pisidia

4. Myra

5. Seleucia

6. Antioch in Syria

7. Daphne, location unknown.

PART TWO

The Acts of Paul and Thecla

Notes on the Translation

This translation employs modern idiomatic English. It strives not only for an accurate translation but also for one that reflects the social and stylistic levels of the Greek version. The Acts of Paul and Thecla was written in koine or common Greek. Its style is paratactic. Connections between sentences and paragraphs are made by "and" with little subordination. The constant repetition of "and" in English style is boring, so we have varied the connective, but tried to mimic the paratactic feel.

Lipsius and Bonnet, *Acta Apostolorum Apocryha*, originally published 1891–1903, remains the only critical edition and formed the basis for our translation. Barrier in his doctoral dissertation on the Acts of Paul and Thecla thoroughly reexamined not only the Greek manuscript tradition, but also those in other ancient languages, especially Coptic.[1] Pervo, *The Acts of Paul*, also examined this same evidence. He is especially good on the variations found in the manuscript tradition. But more importantly, reconstructing an original text is not possible because the manuscript tradition was never fixed. We have carefully considered the suggestions and recommendations of Barrier and Pervo in arriving at our translation. For those interested in the intricacies of the textual issues, Barrier and Pervo provide a good guide. Barrier is more conservative in his judgments, while Pervo is too confident in his ability to reconstruct an original text.

There are two numbering systems in place. The traditional manuscript numbering system starts with 1 and numbers the paragraphs for both stories sequentially through 43. Lipsius and Bonnet introduced chapter numbers into the Acts of Paul. The first Thecla story became chapter 3 and the second one chapter 4. In our translation we have provided both systems for easy reference to other authors who may use one or the other numbering system. 3.2 refers to the second paragraph in chapter 3 or the

1. Published as Barrier, *The Acts of Paul and Thecla*.

second paragraph in the old manuscript numbering system. 4.2 (27) refers to chapter four, paragraph two in the modern system or paragraph 27 in the sequential manuscript numbering system.

Translation and Commentary

Iconium[1]

House of Onesiphorus 3.1–4

3.1 *After fleeing Antioch, on his way to Iconium, Paul was travelling with Demas and Hermogenes, a blacksmith, who were two-faced flatterers, pretending to be devoted to him. Paul, focusing on the goodness done by the Anointed, did not reprove them but gave them his full attention, so that he made sweet tasting to them all the Oracles of the Master, and the birth and resurrection of the Beloved, and the great deeds of the Anointed, as they were revealed word by word to him.*

2 Now a certain man named Onesiphorus, upon hearing that Paul was on his way to Iconium, went out with his sons, Simmias and Zeno, and his wife, Lectra, to welcome him into his house. For Titus had given him a detailed description of what Paul looked like. For he didn't know Paul by sight, but only by reputation within the community.

3 Then he set out on the imperial highway to Lystra, and he stood around waiting for him, while he scanned passers-by according to the description provided by Titus. He saw Paul coming, a short man, bald, bowlegged, fit, with knitted brows, a nose a bit too long, brimming with good will. Sometimes he looked like a man, while at other times he had the face of an angel.

4 And Paul smiled when he saw Onesiphorus. Then Onesiphorus said, "Welcome, slave of the blessed God." And Paul said, "God's favor is with you and your house."

But jealousy was aroused in Demas and Hermogenes, and their two-facedness worsened. Then Demas said, "Don't we belong to the blessed One?

1. APTh begins with chapter 3 of the Acts of Paul.

35

Why didn't you welcome us?" And Onesiphorus said, "I didn't see in you the fruit of justice. But if you're such, come into my house and be refreshed."

Commentary

3.1 This paragraph introduces the first group of characters and situates the story geographically.

Antioch is probably Antioch in Syria, a major city and mentioned once in Galatians 2:11 as a place of major Pauline activity, frequently in Acts of the Apostles, and once in 2 Timothy 3:11. Iconium was a large trading city located inland at the foot of the Taurus Mountains about 120 miles from the Mediterranean. It was a stop on the trade route between Antioch and Ephesus. After Paul's preaching was rejected in Antioch, "they [Paul and Barnabas] shook the dust off their feet in protest against them, and went to Iconium" (Acts 13:51). This verse in Acts probably suggested the introduction to this episode and was added by the author/editor to integrate the Acts of Paul and Thecla (hereafter APTh) into the larger composition of the Acts of Paul. Antioch, Lystra, and Iconium are linked together in Acts and 2 Timothy.

First up is Paul, who is never referred to as "apostle" in the APTh, although some manuscripts have introduced that title. He gets no introduction because in the Acts of Paul he was already the known hero. Later in 3:15 Thamyris, Thecla's betrothed, calls him a foreigner and the crowd charges him as a magician. In 3:14 and 17 Demas and Hermogenes refer to him as an adherent of the Anointed (*christianos*).

Paul's two travelling companions, Demas and Hermogenes, are introduced as "two-faced flatterers." The greetings at the conclusions in Philemon 24 and Colossians 4:14 mention Demas as one of Paul's co-workers. Colossians is not one of Paul's authentic letters. Second Timothy 4:10 identifies Demas as one who has deserted Paul and is "in love with this present world." Also 2 Timothy 1:15 cites Hermogenes as among those in Asia Minor who have turned away from Paul. Demas and Hermogenes function as a single character in opposition to Paul—why then are they his travel companions? Their behavior also contrasts with Onesiphorus.

Onesiphorus occurs twice in 2 Timothy, which locates him in Rome (1:16) and his family in Ephesus (4:19). Demas, Hermogenes, and Onesiphorus point to a connection to 2 Timothy. There are several possible explanations. 1) The APTh knows 2 Timothy. 2) The author/editor of the Acts of Paul drew upon 2 Timothy to create an introduction to incorporate the Thecla stories into this new work. 3) Both 2 Timothy and the APTh draw on the same common background of traditions about Paul. At this point in the narrative there is no clear way to resolve this issue. According to the hypothesis developed in "Thecla in Context" above, we favor option 2.

Titus was a companion of Paul, mentioned in 2 Corinthians and Galatians, as well as once in 2 Timothy. He is the imaginary addressee of the pseudo-Paul letter Titus.

While *christos* is traditionally transliterated as "Christ," "Anointed" is the correct translation. Israel anointed its kings with oil, a rite unknown among Greeks and Romans. "Anointed" accents the Jewish heritage of the title, while the transliteration "Christ" erroneously Christianizes the title.

Categories drawn from the oral tradition describe Paul's preaching about the Anointed. The Oracles of the Master refer to the oral sayings. "Birth and resurrection" strike our ears as strange, instead of the stereotyped phrase "death and resurrection." The alternative phrasing points to the fluid nature of an oral tradition, which is not fixed. "Great deeds" are the miracles. All of this was revealed to Paul. The tradition is oral and piecemeal, not part of a written gospel tradition. Compare with 3.5 below.

2 The householder Onesiphorus offers hospitality to the itinerant preacher Paul. Such hospitable householders formed the backbone of itinerant missionary activity, so common among the early Jesus associations.

Onesiphorus lives in Iconium as a householder with a house, sons, and a wife. Notice the order—sons, then wife. This description of the household assumes a community of the Anointed already exists in Iconium in his house, at odds with the story of Paul's founding of that community in Acts 13:51—14:6.

The Greek literally reads that Onesiphorus did not know Paul "by flesh but only by spirit." What does "by spirit" mean? It might mean "by revelation," but that seems unlikely. Since Onesiphorus learns what Paul looks like from Titus, it probably refers to Paul's reputation within the community.

3 Augustus built a highway between Iconium and Lystra, although no evidence exists of it being called an imperial road.

The APTh furnishes the earliest description of Paul and it stuck.[2] The iconography of Paul always pictures him as bald or balding.[3] The earliest

2. This is the only description of an apostle or Jesus before the fourth century.

3. See János Bollók, "The Description of Paul" for an excellent discussion of the

extant image of Paul from the fourth century in the Catacomb of Tecla (the Latin spelling) clearly exhibits a bald Paul with pointed beard.[4]

4 In the address of his authentic letters, Paul twice refers to himself as "a slave of the Anointed" (Romans 1:1; Galatians 1:10). The use of master/slave language in communities of the Anointed was common, but often disappears in translations under the cover of the euphemisms "Lord" and "servant," less offensive words. Early followers of Master Jesus Anointed were well aware of the scandal of the word slave, realized Jesus had died a slave's death, and accepted the term for themselves.

The introduction of Demas and Hermogenes is forced and interrupts the narrative flow, indicating possible editorial addition. These characters continue in their role of opposition to Paul, an expected theme in a romance story.

Paul's Message 3.5–6

3.5 *Upon entering Onesiphorus' house, there was great rejoicing, while squatting down on the floor, breaking bread, and the announcement of God's message about self-control and resurrection.*

Paul said,

'Congratulations to those whose motives are pure, for they will see God.

Congratulations to those who keep the flesh chaste, for they will be God's temple.

Congratulations to those who practice self-discipline, for God will speak to them.

Congratulations to those who are not lined up with this world, for they will be very pleasing to God.

Congratulations to those who, having wives, do not possess them, for they will be heirs of God.

Congratulations to those who fear God, for they will become heavenly beings with God.

6 *Congratulations to those who tremble at God's Oracles, for they will be comforted.*

Congratulations to those who have received the wisdom of Jesus Anointed, for they will be called children of the Most High.

---

history of this description.

4 https://www.telegraph.co.uk/news/worldnews/europe/vaticancityandholy-see/5675461/Oldest-image-of-St-Paul-discovered.html/.

Congratulations to those who have guarded their ritual bathing, for they will be refreshed by the father and the son.

Congratulations to those who have advanced in the knowledge of Jesus Anointed, for they will be in the light.

Congratulations to those who have left behind the world's fashions out of love of God, for they will judge the heavenly messengers and will be honored with a seat at the right hand of the Father.

Congratulations to the merciful, for they will receive mercy and not see the bitter day of judgment.

Congratulations to virgins whose bodies are very pleasing to God and will not lose the reward for their purity. For the father's word will accomplish salvation in them on the day of his son, and they shall rest forever and ever."

Commentary

5 The breaking of the bread and the announcement of God's message takes place in a house community. Wine is unmentioned. This is a meal and should be viewed as such and not converted to a ritual, typical of later Christian practice. Community life in the APTh centers around the household.

"Self-control and resurrection" summarizes the announcement of God's message, which remains the consistent message throughout the APTh, somewhat different from a more expansive expression at 3:1 above.

Paul begins his preaching in the house. About the audience or its size, the narrator offers no information. Paul begins with a group of beatitudes. Jesus' first sermon in the Gospel of Matthew begins with beatitudes and Paul's first beatitude quotes the sixth beatitude of the Sermon on the Mount (Matthew 5:8). This provides strong evidence that the author knows the Gospel of Matthew, since that beatitude is unique to that gospel.

The first beatitude sets the theme that the remaining beatitudes elaborate. Most deal with self-control. Only beatitudes 6, 7, 11, and 12 do not. None directly deals with resurrection.

The fifth beatitude does not forbid or disapprove of marriage, but it rewards couples who live as though not married. This is the consistent position of the APTh.

6 "Ritual bathing" traditionally is transliterated as "baptism." Bathing is a socially important act in Jewish, as well as Roman worlds. The many public baths found at archaeological sites attest to its importance. Baptism for modern Christians is a sacrament divorced from bathing.

While there is no direct mention of resurrection, the final three beatitudes deal with the postmortem situation.

Whether the beatitudes are the whole of Paul's speech or just the beginning is unclear. While not a realistic representation of Paul's preaching, it does indicate the themes of Paul's preaching according to the APTh.

The Virgin Thecla 3.7

3.7 *Now while Paul was declaring these congratulations in the presence of the gathering in Onesiphorus' house, a certain virgin by the name of Thecla, whose mother was Theokleia and who was promised in marriage to Thamyris, sat at a nearby window in the house night and day listening to the words being spoken by Paul about purity. Now she did not turn away from the window but followed every word with overwhelming joy and trust. But when she saw many other women and virgins going into the place where Paul was, she too yearned for the high honor of standing face to face with Paul to hear the word about the Anointed. For she as yet didn't even have an impression of what Paul looked like, but only had heard the message.*

Commentary

7 The heroine and Paul's romantic partner in this romance comes on the scene. She is Thecla the virgin, which functions as a title. Her family consists of her mother Theokleia and her betrothed Thamyris. Theokleia means "glory of god" and Thecla is its shortened form. So, Thecla and her mother share the same name, very common in the ancient world.

Thecla sits in her house at the window listening to Paul preaching in Onesiphorus' house. She hangs on every word, night and day. That would imply that Paul preached for many nights and days. This exaggeration typifies romances. What attracts Thecla is Paul's preaching on purity. A fresco of Thecla at the window while Paul is preaching was found in a seventh century grotto in Ephesus, Turkey.[5]

---

5. The image and explanation of the archaeological site can be found at https://www.nasscal.com/materiae-apocryphorum/grotto-of-saint-paul/.

Hearing without seeing occurs as an important theme in the oral cultural of the early followers of Jesus. In John 20:16, Mary Magdalene sees Jesus but thinks he is the gardener. She only recognizes him when he speaks her name.

Why would Paul's teaching on purity and continence attract a virgin like Thecla? Her mother is appalled. Pregnancy and childbirth were dangerous and therefore sex was always risky for a female. Marriage greatly limited a woman's freedom. She became the property of her husband. Often there was a considerable age difference between the husband and the wife. Until the advent of modern medicine, this remained the situation. Emily Dickenson's and her sister's choice not to marry should be viewed in this light. A life without marriage held many attractions, so many that the emperor Augustus passed legislation mandating it.[6]

"Gathering" is usually translated "church," but that word is too formal, official, and ecclesiastical for this context. The gathering is in a house, the fundamental social and communal element of the early Jesus Anointed groups.

Theokleia and Thamyris 3.8–10

3.8 *Since she wouldn't leave the window, her mother sent for Thamyris. He eagerly came as if receiving her on their wedding day.*

Then Thamyris said to Theokleia, "Where's my Thecla?"

So Theokleia said, "I have some unexpected news for you, Thamyris. For three days and three nights Thecla hasn't risen from the window, neither to eat nor drink, but gazes as if at a wonderous sight. She's crazy for a foreign guy whose teaching is wily and bizarre. I'm amazed at how a virgin's sense of shame can be so deeply disturbed."

9 *"Thamyris, this man will disrupt the citizens of Iconium, as well as your Thecla. For all the women and youths are flocking to him and being taught by him. 'It is necessary,' he says, 'to fear the one and only God and to live chastely.'*

Just like being caught in a spider's web, so my daughter is under the sway to a new desire and dreadful passion. For she stares intently at what has

---

6. The discussion of this is extensive. See Galinsky, "Augustus' Legislation on Morals and Marriage," 126–44; also Grubbs, "Singles, Sex and Status in the Augustan Marriage Legislation," 105–24.

been said by him. And the virgin is trapped. But go and speak to her, for she is betrothed to you."

10 *When he got there, while loving her and also fearing that she was out of her mind, Thamyris said, "Thecla, you're promised to me in marriage, so why do you remain sitting in this way? And what kind of frenzy has gripped you to the point of being out of your mind? Return to your Thamyris and be ashamed."*

Now her mother also would say, "Child, why are you sitting looking downcast and making no answer, but looking so stricken?" And everyone was weeping bitterly—Thamyris for his missing wife, Theokleia for her child, and the female servants for their mistress. Therefore, the house was overcome in the confusion of mourning. Even while all these things were happening, Thecla didn't turn away, but kept rapturously focusing on the message of Paul.

Commentary

8 The romance plot now comes explicitly into play. Thecla has been at the window for three nights and days, a clear reference to the resurrection. She is clearly entranced, bewitched, and falling in love. In 3:7 she desires the honor of seeing Paul face to face, while her mother complains that as a virgin, she should exhibit the appropriate shame. By shame Theokleia does not mean guilt, but the shame proper to a female that protects male honor. Since Thecla and Thamyris are engaged, her falling for Paul is a direct threat to Thamyris's claim on her and his honor. The exaggeration in the length of time Thecla has been at the window and not eating heightens the intensity of her attraction to Paul.

9 Theokleia expands the danger beyond Thecla to all the women and youths. Paul is challenging marriage, a primary imperative for women in the Roman Empire. Augustus issued extensive legislation requiring marriage for men and women of Thecla's social class and this legislation, while controversial, was enforced by the emperors.[7] "The one and only God" is a Jewish expression, which stresses Paul's foreignness, a fact that Theokleia had raised in the previous verse.

Thecla is depicted as in love, trapped in a spider's web. Her behavior runs directly contrary to the warning in 2 Timothy 2:22: "Shun youthful

---

7. Lefkowitz and Fant, *Women's Life*, has an excellent collection of texts related to this topic.

passions and pursue righteousness, faith, love, and peace, along with those who call on the Lord from a pure heart."

10 Thamyris repeats the theme that Thecla is bewitched or crazy and should be ashamed. Honor/shame is a major theme and value in Greco-Roman culture. Thecla's falling in love with Paul challenges the honor of Thamyris. She should exhibit a virgin's proper shame that would protect Thamyris' honor.

The whole household is thrown into disarray over Thecla's behavior, while she continues "rapturously focusing on the message of Paul." In the terms of the romance novel, she is falling in love.

The social categorization is interesting. Thamyris weeps "for his missing wife, Theokleia for her child, and female servants for their mistress." The Greek for "female servants" indicates that they are young, enslaved females who would have served and attended Thecla. Thecla is not only a slave of God, but also enmeshed in an enslaving culture.

Thamyris's Plot 3.11–15

3.11 *Quickly getting up, Thamyris went out into the street and closely studied those coming and going to see Paul. And he saw two men arguing bitterly with each other. So, he said to them, "You there, tell me, who are you and who's that person with you inside who's leading astray the hearts of young men and charming virgins, so that they won't get married but remain as they are? I promise to give you a whole lot of money if you tell me about him. For I'm among the prominent men of this city."*

12 *And Demas and Hermogenes said to him, "As to the first question, we don't who he is. And as to the second he deprives youths of maidens and virgins of husbands, saying, 'Unless you remain pure and do not defile the flesh, but keep pure, there is no resurrection for you.'"*

13 *Thamyris said to them, "Come over to my house, good fellows, and take some refreshment with me." So, they left for a very expensive dinner and a whole lot of wine and lavish surroundings and a splendid table. And Thamyris offered them drink, because loving Thecla, he wished to gain her as his wife. Now during the meal Thamyris said, "Good fellows, tell me, what's he teaching, so that I too may know? For I am really upset about Thecla, because she so loves the foreigner, and I am being robbed of a wedding night."*

14 *Then Demas and Hermogenes said, "Bring him to the attention of the governor Castelius on the charge that he is persuading the crowds to turn to*

the new teachings of those who adhere to the Anointed. And that way, you'll destroy him and get Thecla for your wife. Now we'll give you the inside info on what he says about resurrection: it has already happened in our children."

15 *When Thamyris heard these things from them, and full of envy and an angry heart, he got up and went to Onesiphorus' house with the rulers and public officials and a crowd with clubs, saying to Paul, "You have so corrupted the city of the Iconians and the one promised to me that she no longer desires me. Let's go to the governor Castelius." And the whole crowd would shout, "Away with the magician. For he's deceived every last one of our wives." And the crowd was convinced.*

Commentary

11 Thamyris takes action. After observing those coming and going from Onesiphorus' house, he questions two men he finds arguing in the street. These two, as the villains in the set piece, are arguing bitterly with each other. What they are arguing about is unimportant, but they are living up to their characterization. Thamyris goes straight to what he sees as the fundamental issue with Paul's teaching. Paul leads astray young men and charms virgins so that they will not get married. Since Augustus, the Roman Empire enforced policies to encourage and foster marriage, especially among the upper class. Therefore, Paul's teaching is political and subverts the values of the Empire.

Until this point in the story, Thamyris' status had not been revealed. He is wealthy and a prominent citizen of Iconium. Wealth and prominence go together. From the point of view of Theokleia, he is a desirable catch.

12 Demas and Hermogenes, true to their character, deny knowing who Paul is. Their summary of Paul's teaching ties the teaching about purity to resurrection, reinforcing the summary of Paul's teaching in 3:5.

13 The lavish spread at Thamyris' dinner contrasts with the simple bread at Onsesiphorus' welcoming of Paul. Paul is a foreigner, Thamyris a prominent citizen. Thecla loves Paul and Thamyris is "being robbed of a wedding night." The story lines up with a series of contrasts.

14 Demas and Hermogenes propose a plot that will eliminate Paul. Thamyris should denounce Paul before the governor because "he is persuading the crowds to turn to the new teachings of those who adhere to the Anointed." "Those who adhere to the Anointed" or "these who belong to the party of the Anointed" are accurate translations of *christianoi*, traditionally transliterated "Christians."[8] The Anointed is the Jewish messiah. So pledging allegiance to a Jewish messiah betrays the allegiance due the Roman Emperor. Translating the word as "Anointed" makes the charge of treason clear.

Martyrdom was a major element in the formation of Christian identity. Although later Christians exaggerated its frequency and pervasiveness, martyrdom nevertheless posed a real danger.

For Thamyris the treasonable offense was Paul's preaching calling for abstinence from marriage, which would rob him of the wife who was his due. That young women were not available for marriage provokes outrage because it attacks the very patriarchal structure of empire. Demas and Hermogenes are recommending a different tack. Thamyris should denounce Paul as one who belongs to the party of the Anointed. That will get him killed.

In their summary of Paul's teaching about resurrection, it has already happened. This is another connection to the Pastorals which warn about such a teaching in 2 Timothy 2:18. But nowhere else in the APTh is the resurrection understood as present.

Finally, this scene with Demas and Hermogenes appears to have been inserted when the APTh was incorporated into the Acts of Paul. It is extraneous because Thamyris does not follow their advice!

15 The novelistic character of the narrative is evident when, without effort, Thamyris rouses the city's rulers, public officials, and a crowd to go to Onesiphorus' house to confront Paul. Before the governor, Paul is denounced as a magician because "he's deceived every last one of our wives." Demas and Hermogenes' suggestion of accusing Paul of belonging to the adherents of the Anointed plays no role in the narrative.

There are strong parallels to the trial of Jesus before Pilate and Paul's trials in Acts. The crowd is stirred up (Mark 15:11), comes with clubs (Mark 14:48 and parallels), and the charge of magic (Acts 19:13–20). Corrupting the youth was the same charge as against Socrates in his trial.

Paul's Trial 3.16–17

3.16 *And standing before the judgment bench, Thamyris cried out in horrible distress, "Proconsul, this very man, we don't know where he comes from and*

---

8. Vearncombe, *After Jesus*, chap. 2, for a discussion of why translating *christianoi* makes more sense than transliterating.

45

he doesn't allow virgins to marry. Make him tell you why he teaches these things."

But Demas and Hermogenes said to Thamyris, "Say that he belongs to the party of the Anointed, and you will destroy him."

Now the governor stood his ground and called Paul forward and said to him, "Who are you and what are you teaching? For you're facing grave charges."

17 Paul raised his voice saying, "If today I'm being examined on what I teach, listen up, proconsul. The living God, the God of vengeance, [a jealous God,] a God who wants for nothing, that God longs for the salvation of people. He has sent me, so that I should tear them away from corruption and uncleanliness and every lust and death, so that they will no longer go astray. Therefore, God sent his own child, whom I announce as good news and teach people to hope in that one who alone felt deeply for a world gone astray, so that people may not be under judgment any longer but might have confidence in and fear of God and a knowledge of reverence and awe and love of truth. Therefore, if I teach the things revealed to me by God, what harm am I doing, proconsul?"

But upon hearing this, the governor ordered Paul bound and thrown in prison, until he had the leisure to hear his case more carefully.

Commentary

16 Thamyris charges that Paul is a foreigner, not from Iconium, which indicates how important local identities were in the Roman Empire. It is hard to determine which of Thamyris' charges is more important: that Paul is a foreigner or that he is persuading the virgins not to marry.

Again, Demas and Hermogenes interrupt the narrative flow to bring forward the charge that Paul is an adherent of the Anointed, but Thamyris does not follow their lead and the proconsul does not ask about it. It appears inserted.

The proconsul's question concerning how many charges are brought against Paul finds a parallel in Jesus' trial before Pilate in Mark 15:4 and Matthew 27:13.

17 Paul raising his voice signals his experience as a rhetor. In addressing the governor, Paul uses the more formal title proconsul. The piling on of titles for the deity is common in traditional Mediterranean religious address but contrary to Jesus' command in Matthew 6:7 not to "heap up empty phrases."

The first of God's titles, "the living God," a Jewish title, parallels Paul's preaching in Lystra when the local priests attempt to offer them sacrifice. ""Friends, why are you doing this? We are mortals just like you, and we bring you good news, that you should turn from these worthless things to the living God, who made the heaven and the earth and the sea and all that is in them" (Acts 14:15). This ties Paul's preaching to resurrection. The good news of Paul's preaching is the liberation from impurity. This continues the summary of Paul's teaching in 3.5 above. Thecla in her own trial refers to herself as "a slave of the living God" (4.12).

Jesus Anointed is referred to as "child," not the more normal "son." How God's sending his child fits into the plan of salvation is left vague. It is unclear to whom "that one who alone felt deeply for a world gone astray" refers: the child or God? While resurrection and purity are prominent, the child's death goes unmentioned. Salvation, which is liberation from death caused by uncleanliness, is achieved through teaching. Confidence, fear, and knowledge are linked together.

Paul concludes, "I teach the things revealed to me by God," as was the case in 3.1. The revelation comes directly to Paul, not through or by the child.

As with the governor Felix in Acts 24:25, he imprisons Paul to questioned him another day. The governor's depiction is neutral, or possibly positive towards Paul. He does not rush to judgment and resists the crowd.

Thecla Seeks Paul 3.18–19

3.18 *Then that night, Thecla, taking off her bracelets, bribed the gatekeeper to open the door for her. Then she went to the prison. And giving the prison guard a silver mirror, she entered Paul's prison cell. After sitting down at his feet, she heard the great things of God. And Paul feared no one, but he behaved openly as a really empowered citizen. Now her confidence grew as she was kissing his chains.*

19 *But Thecla was being sought by her own people and Thamyris. They searched through the streets for her like she was lost. And one of the gatekeeper's fellow slaves informed them that she had gone out at night. Then they questioned the gatekeeper, and he said that she had gone to the imprisoned foreigner. And they left and found matters just as he had described them, with* *her twisted up in the chains of love. After leaving that place, they stirred up the crowd and told the governor everything.*

Commentary

18 Thecla bribes both the gatekeeper, a slave of her own house, and the prison guard. This first meeting with her lover takes place in prison. But it is not her love that grows in this romance but her confidence as she kisses his chains. In romance novels, the lovers are often separated and reunited in prison.

The description of Paul acting as a real citizen of a free city is unexpected. It implies a strong contrast with his self-description as slave of God. The paradox: a slave of God is truly free.

19 Thecla's search for Paul is replayed when her own people and Thamyris go in search of her. This replay drags out the plot. When discovered in Paul's prison cell, she is "twisted up in the chains of love," following the plot of a romance tale.

Judgment 3.20–21a

3.20 *So, he ordered Paul to be brought before the judgment bench. But Thecla was rolling around on the ground where Paul had sat teaching while in prison. And the governor also ordered her to be brought before the judgment bench. And she came rejoicing very exceedingly.*

Then when Paul had been led out, the crowd screamed at the top of their voices, "He's a magician. Away with him!" The governor eagerly heard from Paul about the holy works of the Anointed.

After having taken counsel, he called for Thecla, saying "Why are you refusing to marry Thamyris according to the law of the Iconians?" She stood her ground, gazing intently at Paul, all the while making no answer.

Theokleia, her mother, cried out saying, "Burn the lawless one! Burn her in this theater the one who refused to marry, so that all those women who have been taught by this one may be afraid."

21a *Then the governor was deeply moved. And after scourging Paul, he expelled him from the city. But Thecla he condemned to be burned.*

Commentary

20 How to understand Thecla's rolling around on the ground is unclear. The verb could also mean groveling. Does this signal her falling in love or is she grieving over Paul being taken away?

When Thamyris with Thecla's household discovers her with Paul in prison, they stir up the crowd and alert the governor. Paul's trial resumes, while Thecla remains in prison. Then the governor brings Thecla to the trial, which she is most happy to do. The narrative order is confusing. Why was Thecla left in the prison cell and not brought before the governor at the same time as Paul? Does Thecla rejoice when brought before the governor because she is joining Paul or because she thinks she will die a martyr? Or both?

While the crowd charges Paul with being a magician as they did in 3.15, the governor is positively disposed towards him and hears his preaching, a theme often encountered in the trials in the Acts of the Apostles, e.g., Acts 23:22. But the governor takes a different tack towards Thecla. He questions her about Thamyris' charge of refusing to marry him and asks why she violates the law of the Iconians, which keeps the focus local. Nevertheless, the charge of refusing to marry strikes at the heart of the Empire. It is truly treasonous. Continence is not simply about rejecting sex and marriage but is also a political statement. It goes in the face of imperial legislation (see Commentary 3.7, 9 above). That is why the governor expels Paul from the city but condemns Thecla to death. A woman renouncing marriage also has a political and revolutionary dimension in the ancient world.

The trial at no point picks up on the suggestion of Demas and Hermogenes that Paul be charged as an adherent of the Anointed. Thecla remains silent like Jesus at his trial, but continues to gaze at Paul, the object of her love.

Theokleia turns viciously against her daughter, remaining Thecla's adversary in the romance with Paul. The mother supports the primacy of marriage and calls for her daughter's execution as a threat to the common good. She represents stability; Thecla represents revolution.

Execution 3.21b–22

3.21b *So immediately the governor got up and went to the theater, and the whole crowd as though driven by necessity went along to see the spectacle.*

Thecla, like a lamb in the desert looking around for the shepherd, was seeking Paul. While looking into the crowd, she saw the Master, sitting where Paul would. And she said, "While I'm finding this so difficult to endure, Paul came to keep watch over me." With an intense gaze she hung on to him, as he slipped off into the sky.

22 The young boys and virgins brought straw and firewood to burn Thecla. But when she was brought in naked, the governor wept and was amazed at the force of her presence. Then the executioners stacked up the wood and ordered her to climb up onto the fire. Making the sign of the cross, she climbed up on the pile. They set it on fire. And while the roaring blaze spread, the fire did not touch her. For the compassionate God made a rumbling below the ground and a cloud overshadowed spilling forth with water and hail. Then all its contents rained down, putting many at risk of death and quenching the fire. So, Thecla was saved.

Commentary

21b Even though the governor is deeply moved, he goes ahead with Paul's expulsion from the city and Thecla's condemnation. In Jesus' trial, Pilate was afraid of the crowd (John 19:8). While not unheard of, it would be unusual for a woman of Thecla's high rank to be publicly executed. In the governor's eyes, Thecla's crime, rejecting marriage, is greater than Paul's. Hers is the more profound threat to the empire.[9]

While the lamb/shepherd metaphor recalls the biblical metaphor of the good shepherd, here the shepherd is Paul, not Jesus. Her vision reinforces her focus on Paul. The Master and Paul are interchangeable. Paul comes to her aid. The Greek literally reads: "She saw the Master sitting as Paul." It has several possible meanings. She saw the Master where she expected to see Paul, or she saw the Master and he looked like Paul. In either case, the meaning is clear. In her vision, the Master and Paul are identical.

22 This is the first of two execution or martyrdom scenes in the APTh. Both scenes are dramatic, but this one has several exceptional elements. Normally an execution of a woman of Thecla's status would be by beheading. Death by fire is particularly degrading and a gruesome way to die. It heightens the tension. The very group, young boys and virgins, to whom Paul's teaching had appealed bring the fuel for her death. Her nudity is

---

9. Streete, *Redeemed Bodies*, 82–83, emphasizes this point.

likewise exceptional, but the governor's reaction stresses her beauty and attractiveness, a repeated theme in the APTh.

This passage marks the earliest mention of the sign of the cross, although how to understand the gesture is not clear. It might mean that she held her arms extended. Although Jesus on the cross is not mentioned, it is implied—the only mention of the cross in the APTh. Thecla herself climbs onto the pyre, underlining her independence even in a time of great trial. The whole set up of this scene points to Thecla's independence and isolation. No one is standing with her, not even her "lover" Paul.

The martyrdom of Blandina in Lyons in 177 CE resembles Thecla's. After various tortures, "Blandina was hung on a post . . . . She looked as if she was hanging in the form of a cross." Those who were suffering with her, "saw with their outward eyes in the person of their sister the One who was crucified for them."[10]

As the blaze roars, it does not touch her. A pun may be intended here. The Greek word used for "touch" can also mean "to set off a fire." The fire's not consuming her is the first of several amazing acts in this short scene. Below and above the earth the compassionate God acts. An earthquake shakes the ground, and a cloud pours forth water and hail that quenches the fire and saves Thecla. At the same time, it threatens the spectators' lives. The gods saving the pure maiden is a common theme in romance novels of the period.

The scene ends abruptly. "So, Thecla was saved" by her compassionate God. The reader is left with many unanswered questions. What's to happen to Thecla? Does she go free? If so, where does she go? How does she get clothes? How many of those cheering her death were killed? But the abruptness accents a compassionate God saving Thecla. All else is set aside.

"Saved" is a resonant word. Thecla is saved from the fire, but the earthquake and water and hail raining down has the look and feel of an apocalyptic judgment scene. This suggests that "saved" should be understood in a deeper sense. God has saved Thecla. She is clearly marked out.

In a Tomb 3.23

3.23 *Paul was fasting with Onesiphorus and his wife and their children in an empty tomb on the road between Iconium and Daphne. After many days of fasting had passed, the children said to Paul, "We're hungry." And they didn't*

10. Eusebius, *The History of the Church*, 5.41.

have any money to buy food. For Onesiphorus had left the things of the world to follow Paul with his whole household. Then Paul took off his coat and said, "Go, child. Buy a lot of bread and bring it back."

But as the child was buying the bread, he saw his neighbor Thecla and said to Thecla, "Where're you going?" So she said, "I'm looking for Paul because I've been saved from the fire." Then the child said, "Come on, I'll lead you to him. For he sighs deeply for you. And he's been praying and fasting for the past six days."

Commentary

23 Narrative abruptness persists. Instead of explaining Thecla's situation, the scene shifts to Paul and Onesiphorus and his family in an empty tomb outside of Iconium,[11] from which Paul had been expelled. How the household of Onesiphorus and his family got there is unexplained. The abruptness of both the end of Thecla's near martyrdom and the shift to Paul's exile in the tomb drives the narrative forward at a quick pace and keeps the focus on the action.

Does the empty tomb have a double meaning? Does it stand in for Jesus' tomb and foreshadow a resurrection, or does it point to the characters' homeless situation? Homelessness and itinerancy are signature characteristics of the Anointed's missionaries. Because Onesiphorus and his family have left everything to follow Paul, they do not even have enough money to feed their children.

When the children complain of hunger, Paul gives one of them his coat and sends the child off to buy bread, emphasizing the group's poverty. They are down to the clothes on their backs or maybe Paul's is the last coat. The coat could be a reference to 2 Timothy 4:13, but more likely it recalls the missionary commission of Jesus: "Don't get gold or silver or copper coins for spending money, don't take a knapsack for the road, or two shirts, or sandals, or a staff; for the worker deserves to be fed" (Matthew 10:9–10).

The child encounters Thecla on the way to buy bread. Thecla summarizes her story as seeking Paul and being saved from the fire, again distilling the action to its essential points. At the scene's end the child explains the reason for Paul's fasting. The fasting has been going on for six days and leaves the question unanswered as to what Thecla has been doing for those six days. Wandering around the city?

11. The location of Daphne is unknown and many manuscripts omit it.

Reunion 3.24–25a

3.24 *Then she came upon Paul at the tomb squatting on the floor, and praying, and saying, "Father of the Anointed, do not let the fire touch Thecla, but be with her, because she is yours."*

But standing behind, she cried out, "Father, maker of the sky and earth, Father of your beloved child Jesus Anointed, I praise you because you have saved me from the fire so that I may see Paul."

Then standing up Paul saw her and said, "God, knower of hearts, Father of our Master Jesus Anointed, I praise you because what I asked for, you've speedily granted me."

25a *Now within the tomb was a whole lot of love, with Paul and Onesiphorus and the others rejoicing. They had five loaves of bread and vegetables and water. So they celebrated the Anointed's holy deeds.*

Commentary

24 In the standard romance novel, now is the expected reunion of the separated and tested lovers in which they will exchange vows in a temple. The reunion scene has a nice ABA balance, with God addressed as "father" in all three elements.

Squatting is not the normal posture for praying but standing with hands extended. Literally, the Greek reads "who had bent his knees." This phrase is unusual. The normal phrase in the New Testament is "put one's knee [on the ground] (Acts 7:60), based on the image of making homage to one's superior. That may be the meaning here. But poor people squat on the floor. Either reading is possible.

Paul has been praying for six days. He acknowledges that Thecla belongs to God.

Thecla's prayer doubles the reference to God as father. First, she addresses the father maker of sky and earth, recalling the apocalyptic earthquake and outpouring from the sky that saved her from the fire. Second, she addresses the father of the "child Jesus Anointed." Jesus was referred to as child in 3:17. While Paul beseeches God, Thecla appropriately offers praise to God for saving her from the fire so she can see Paul, a constant refrain.

Paul in turn addresses God first as knower of hearts. This is one of the strongest pieces of evidence that the author knows the Acts of the Apostles.

This word occurs in Acts 1:24 and 15:8. Paul then addresses God as the father of our Master Jesus Anointed. "Slave" is a primary term for the followers of the anointed in the APTh. When Onesiphorus first meets Paul, he addresses him as "slave of the blessed God." He matches Thecla's praise for God saving her.

25a The eucharist celebrating God saving Thecla is a real meal. There is no mention of a cup, but five loaves of bread, echoing the feeding of the five thousand (Matthew 14:17), vegetables and water. When the Acts of Paul and Thecla were composed, the eucharist was not formalized in ritual.

Paul's Fear 3.25b–26

3.25b *Then Thecla said to Paul, "I'll cut off my hair and follow you wherever you go."*

But he said, "The times are shameful! And you are stunning. Yet another test may leave you worse off than the first and you may not survive but behave like a coward."

So, Thecla said, "Only give me the Anointed's seal, and no test will touch me."

And Paul said, "Thecla, be patient and you will receive the water."

26a *Then Paul sent Onesiphorus and all his family back to Iconium.*

Commentary

Thecla responds to God's saving her by following Paul. She proposes to cut off her hair which can be understood in several ways. To follow Paul, she must be a man. Since travelling with Paul would be dangerous, she must pass as a man. Perhaps Thecla is proposing a way around the command in the canonical version of 1 Corinthians 14:35 in which Paul silences women. But the canonical version of Paul's letters was probably not in circulation at this time and furthermore the APTh shows no knowledge of Paul's letters. More likely, Thecla is acting out Paul's "neither male nor female" (Galatians 3:28). By becoming a male she transcends sex, as in Gospel of Thomas 22: "when you make male and female into a single one, so that the male will not be male nor the female female." In this context continence protests the cultural dominance of patriarchy. This interpretation of Thecla's cutting her hair coheres with the theme of Paul's preaching as portrayed in the APTh.

Her offer to follow Paul wherever he goes recalls the Q-Gospel saying in Luke 9:57: "I'll follow you wherever you go." Following Paul or Jesus could make one homeless. This continues the motif of the interchanging of Paul and Jesus seen previously. She is proposing to become a missionary of the Anointed.

Paul too is impressed with Thecla's beauty and worries that she will fail should another test occur. He is afraid she will act like a coward. The Greek word for "coward" shares the same root (*andreia*) as "courage" or "manliness."[12] Paul clearly underestimates Thecla and she has greater spiritual insight than he. Paul knows that God has saved Thecla but still he hesitates.

Thecla requests the Anointed's seal, while Paul counsels patience, "Wait yet a time for the water." While baptism is clearly implied, the word is not used.

This story ends where it began, with Onesiphorus and his family in Iconium, an inclusion in which ancient audiences delighted. It marks an ending. It is implied that Thecla remains with Paul.

Antioch[13]

Alexander Pursues Thecla 4.1 (26b)

4.1 (26b) *And then Paul took Thecla and went to Antioch. Just as they were entering, a leader of the Syrian community, a certain Alexander, seeing Thecla, fell head over heels in love with her. Now he strongly pressed Paul with money and gifts. But Paul said, "I don't know the woman you're speaking about; she's not mine." But because he was very powerful, he threw his arms around her in the middle of the street.*

But she didn't put up with it but kept seeking Paul. And she protested bitterly, saying, "You don't assault a stranger! Don't overpower God's slave! Among the Iconians I am of the first rank and because I didn't want to marry Thamyris, I was expelled from the city." And after having been accosted by Alexander, she grabbed him by the collar and knocked the laurel leaf crown off his head. So, there she stood triumphant.

---

12. Streete, *Redeemed Bodies*, 85, makes this point.
13. This begins chapter 4 in the Acts of Paul.

Commentary

4.1 (26b) While modern editors mark a sharp break between the Iconium and Antioch stories, the ancient editor who incorporated these two stories into the Acts of Paul made no such clear distinction. The editor employed a paratactic style by which "and" knits each sentence together with little subordination. This compositional method does not denote whether Paul's return to Antioch with Thecla concludes the previous story or begins this one. But the narrative breaks with a change in geography when Paul takes Thecla to Antioch. These two stories surely were separate before their incorporation into the Acts of Paul. The Greek editor ran the two stories together—an overly simple editorial method. This translation makes a sharp break between the stories honoring the narrative shift. The ancient editor's compositional run–on did not make a break that sharp.

Both the Iconium and Antioch stories follow the same basic pattern. Thecla is sought by an upper-class man, she is arrested, found guilty, and is rescued from execution. The Antioch story is more complex and elaborate than the Iconium story. Thecla is more active and assertive. In Iconium her mother is the principal opponent, while in Antioch she has a female patron, Tryphaena. Paul in Antioch is more problematic, so much so that some think he was added to an original Thecla story.

There were many cities named Antioch in the Roman Empire. Antioch of Pisidia is the most likely reference, which is 95 miles (154 km) east of Iconium. It was a major city lying at the crossroads between the Aegean, Mediterranean, and the Anatolian highlands. The major problem with this suggestion is that Alexander is described as a Syrian, which would argue for Antioch in Syria on the Orontes River. Perhaps this is another example of sloppy editing in joining two different stories together.

The action starts straight off. A high-ranking member of the city falls for Thecla and attempts to buy her or bribe Paul to gain access to her. In response, Paul denies that he knows her and claims she does not belong to him. Interpreting this is difficult. In romance novels, when the couple faces tribulation, one will lie to protect the other. A similar motif occurs in the Abraham and Sarah story (Genesis 20:1–18).[14] But here Paul abandons Thecla. Perhaps Alexander perceives Thecla as a prostitute and Paul as her owner. He bargains for her services or offers to buy her outright.[15]

---

14. Barrier, *The Acts of Paul and Thecla*, 140.

15. Pervo, *The Acts of Paul*, 148.

This makes sense, especially considering Thecla's response, but it does not explain Paul's response. In any event, Paul comes off badly, despite commentators' effort to excuse him. From this point, Paul disappears from the narrative until its end, another reason some suggest that Paul was added to the story by the editor of the Acts of Paul. But if that is the case, it does not explain why the editor would cast Paul in such a bad light.

In what sense is Alexander powerful? Physically or socially? Or both? He feels entitled. This is an attempted rape scene, very different from Thamyris' pursuit of marriage. But Thecla, in contrast to Paul, responds forcefully. She challenges Alexander's lack of hospitality towards a foreigner or stranger. "How dare you attack God's slave!" This is her self-understanding as a follower of Jesus the Anointed. If Alexander had taken her as Paul's slave, hers would be an appropriate and ironic riposte. Finally, she claims to be among the upper crust of the Iconians, an equal of Alexander. The audience learns that, following her escape from the fire, she was expelled from the city.

Then Thecla knocks the crown off Alexander's head. The crown indicates that he has imperial status, so he really is among the elite. Thecla has dishonored Alexander by her attack, which demands a response.

The scene ends with Thecla standing in the street triumphant, a defining image of Thecla in the Antioch story in contrast to her passivity in the Iconium story and in sharp contrast to the two males, Paul and Alexander.

Tryphaena 4.2

4.2 (27) *While both loving her and having been shamed by what happened to him, he dragged her off to the governor. And after confessing that she did these things, he condemned her to the wild beasts, especially since Alexander was going to provide them.*

But the women of the city protested in front of the judgment bench, "Horrible decision, ungodly decision."

When Thecla asked the governor that she might be allowed to protect her purity until she would fight the beasts, a wealthy woman of the imperial family by the name of Tryphaena, who had lost her daughter, took her into her keeping and so gained her as a consolation.

Commentary

2 (27) Though torn between love (lust?) and the insult to his honor, Alexander moves immediately to the governor. The narrative skips over the charge and trial and jumps to the condemnation to death by wild beasts. Again, such a punishment is inappropriate for a woman of Thecla's status, which is why the women, who suddenly appear in the narrative like a Greek chorus, protest. But the governor is persuaded by Alexander and especially his offer to pay for the wild beasts. Paying for the wild animals in a public show is always a major issue because the expense was burdensome and the honor for providing them great.

The story continues to move at a breakneck pace. Since her fight with the beasts will not be for a few days, Thecla asks for a guardian to protect her purity. Purity and its protection is a major theme of the APTh as well as the Acts of Paul. It is unusual to execute a virgin and there are examples of virgins being raped in order to proceed with execution. From an ancient reader's point of view, Thecla's request makes sense.

This brings Tryphaena onto the stage. There was an historical Antonia Tryphaena who was related to the royal family of Thrace, as well as distantly related to several emperors. Tryphaena's status more than balances Alexander's. She also functions as an antitype to Alexander. He is an aggressive male; she a nurturing female. She is both a patroness and a potential mother figure.[16]

Parade 4.3–4

4.3 (28) *At the time the wild beasts were lining up for the parade, they tied her to a fierce lioness and the royal Tryphaena followed after her. And all the while Thecla was seated on the lioness, it was licking her feet. So, the whole crowd was stunned.*

The charge as inscribed read "Temple Robber." The women with children cried out from the upper seats, "O god, an ungodly decision has gone down in this city!"

Now after the parade Tryphaena took her home, for her dead daughter Falconilla in a dream had said to her, "Mother, you will take the abandoned

---

16. Misset-van de Weg, "A Wealthy Woman Named Tryphaena," focuses on the emergence of a Christian form of patronage widespread in the Roman Empire.

stranger Thecla in my place, so that she might pray for me, and I might be taken up to a place of the just ones."

4 (29) After Tryphaena had retrieved her from the parade, she continued to mourn because Thecla was going to face the wild beasts the next morning and felt the same love for her as she did for her own daughter Falconilla. She said, "My second child Thecla, come and pray for my first child, so that she might live forever. For I had this dream."

And without hesitating, she raised her voice and said, "My God, son of the Most High who is in the sky, grant her what she wants, so that her daughter Falconilla may live forever." Upon hearing Thecla pray this way, Tryphaena was overwhelmed with grief realizing how this beauty would be thrown to the wild beasts.

Commentary

3 (28) While the action is fast moving, the depiction of Thecla's punishment is elaborate. It begins with a parade of the victim and wild beasts as a prelude to gladiatorial events. The execution will take place in the arena as part of the games. The gladiatorial aspect was absent in the first execution attempt. Expectations raised by a fierce lioness are immediately contradicted by the animal licking her feet. As in the Iconian execution, things do not go according to plan, or at least the plan of the executioners. Thecla's compassionate God still protects her.

The charge is literally "Temple Robber." Plundering a temple is a sacrilege and so Thecla's crime may be understood as an attack upon the city's gods. The mothers watching take exception to the charge and cry out that the decision is against god. The women are not appealing to the God of Israel or the God of the followers of Jesus, but to the god of their city. It is unfortunate that capitalization carries such a heavy theological and unwarranted weight. The women are sitting in the upper seats, the cheap seats, where the women were required to sit. Roman audiences were strictly segregated by class and then gender. All the women and slaves sat in the distant, upper seats.

Dreams and visions are regular vehicles for revelation throughout all forms of Greco-Roman literature and figure prominently in the later acts of the martyrs. "Abandoned stranger," a strong description, contrasts with Falconilla, a daughter. Thecla has the power to intercede with God. Technically, Falconilla wants to be translated from where she is to the place of the just ones. Greeks and Romans did not view the underworld as a desirable place. But what is envisioned here is unclear. Our understanding of how followers of Jesus Anointed understood what happens after death is vague.

4 (29) Tryphaena, in mourning for her natural daughter, now faces mourning for her adopted daughter. Tryphaena is shifting from patroness/protector to mother.

The addressee of Thecla's prayer is unclear. Is "my God" the son who lives in the sky? Or does this prayer address God and God's son? This second option seems most probable. "Most High" is a traditional title from the Hebrew Scriptures. This is another example of how those who follow Jesus the Anointed view themselves as belonging to the tradition of Israel and adopt that language.

Once again, Thecla's beauty comes to the fore. The various mentions of Tryphaena keep coming back to her mourning, indicating the evitable outcome for Thecla. From Tryphaena's point of view, the beasts will kill Thecla, but the reader knows that Thecla is under God's special protection. This creates narrative tension.

To the Arena 4.5–7

4.5 (30) *At dawn Alexander came to take her away, because he was paying for the games of hunting wild animals, saying, "The governor is in his seat and the crowd is getting into an uproar. Hand over the one condemned to the beasts, so that I can take her away."*

Tryphaena screamed so that he fled. She said, "My household is undergoing a second mourning for Falconilla and no one can help—not my child, for she is dead, nor my kin, for I am a widow. God of Thecla, my child, help Thecla!"

6 (31) *Then the governor sent soldiers to carry Thecla away, but Tryphaena wouldn't get out of the way. But she took her by the hand and led her up, saying, "My daughter Falconilla has departed to the tomb, but you, Thecla, are going to fight the beasts."*

And Thecla wept bitterly and groaned to the Master, saying, "Master, the God whom I trust, to whom I have flown, who rescued me from the fire, grant a reward to Tryphaena who has commiserated with your slave and has kept me pure."

7 (32) *Then there was a noise and a roaring of the beasts and a cry of the citizens and the women who were sitting in their places, saying, "Bring in* *the Temple Robber." While others were shouting, "Wipe out this city for this injustice! Wipe us all out! Proconsul, a bitter spectacle and an evil decision!"*

Commentary

5 (30) This is the second time the narrator notes that Alexander is paying for the wild animals. Previously the governor had agreed to condemn Thecla to the wild beasts because Alexander was willing to bear the expense (4:2).

Tryphaena's response to Alexander's demand to hand over Thecla is to play the poor, abandoned, defenseless widow, a role that ill befits her imperial status. She explicitly addresses the "God of Thecla," indicating that more than one god is in play in the scene. She only knows about Thecla's God from Thecla and that God contrasts with the god she had served.

Once again, a female gets the better of Alexander. This Alexander is in no way great.

6 (31) Resisting Alexander is one thing; resisting the governor is another. The governor has the state's power on his side. Despite Tryphaena's contrast of her daughter who went to a tomb and Thecla who is leaving to fight the beasts, the end result is the same. Both end up in a tomb.

In Thecla's prayer she prays not for herself but for Tryphaena who has protected her purity. The contrast is between her Master, God, who has rescued her before and Thecla, God's slave. She does not call on the Master to rescue her again. Does she want to be martyred? She surely is not trying to escape it. By the mid-second century the debates about the desirability of martyrdom were beginning to heat up.[17]

7 (32) The scene shifts abruptly to the arena where all is chaos. The crowd is divided between its male citizens and its females, apparently sitting in the upper seats (see 4.3). While the grammar is unclear, it appears the men are calling for Thecla to be brought to justice, while the women are protesting in the strongest terms.

In the Arena 4.8–10

4.8 (33) *After being taken from the grasp of Tryphaena, Thecla was stripped naked and given a gladiator's girdle and led into the arena. Then lions and*

17. Perkins, *The Suffering Self.*

61

bears were set upon her, and a fierce lioness, charging, laid down at her feet. But the crowd of women shouted at the top of their voices. When a bear attacked her, then the lioness reacted, faced off, and tore the bear to pieces. And again, one of Alexander's lions which had been trained to fight humans, rushed her and the lioness and lion became entangled, and both were killed. The women mourned all the more because her helper, the lioness, had also died.

9 (34) *Then many more wild beasts are let loose, while she is standing and stretching out her hands in prayer. But when she finished praying, she turned and saw a deep ditch full of water. Therefore, she said, "Now it's the right time to wash myself." And she threw herself into the water, saying, "In the name of Jesus Anointed I cleanse myself on my last day."*

But the women and the whole crowd upon seeing this cried out, saying, "Don't cast yourself into the water," so that even the governor was shedding tears because the seals were going to eat this beautiful young woman. But she threw herself into the water in the name of Jesus Anointed. But after seeing a flash of lightning, the seals bobbed up to the surface dead. Then around her was a cloud of fire, so that neither wild beasts could reach her, nor could she be seen naked.

10 (35) *The women shouted out vehemently, as yet more fierce wild beasts were let loose. And they threw leaves, nard, cassia, amomum, so that they were overwhelmed with the aroma of perfume. All the savage wild beasts, falling back as though asleep, did not touch her.*

Alexander said to the governor, "I have some very fierce bulls; we should bind her to these fighting beasts. And the governor reluctantly permitted it, saying, "Do what you want." And they bound her feet between the bulls, and they shoved red-hot irons on their testicles to provoke them to kill her. As a result, they sprang into action. But the burning flame of fire burnt through the strong ropes, leaving her as though she was not bound.

Commentary

8 (33) The narration quickly glances back to when Thecla was taken from Tryphaena. Her nakedness contrasts with Tryphaena's protection of Thecla's purity. The nature of the undergarment she is given is unclear. Given that she is fighting the wild beasts, a gladiator's girdle is reasonable.[18]

18. We owe this suggestion to Erin Vearncombe, an expert on ancient costume.

Now the action begins. When the lions and bears are set upon her, a lioness defends her, as in 4:3. Alexander appears to be orchestrating the show against Thecla. When the lioness kills a bear, he sends a lion specially trained to kill humans into the fray. Both lioness and lion are killed. All this slaughter is costing Alexander a great deal of money—wild animals were not cheap. The women continue to be on Thecla's side. She is left without protection.

9 (34) Thecla's self-baptism is the action that generated the most controversy about the APTh. It drew Tertullian's scorn (see above, "The Presbyter"). She stands nude, praying with hands extended in the standard Roman way. Such praying women are common in Christian catacombs.[19] The water in the arena was apparently for a water spectacle. Thecla sees the water and decides this is the appropriate time (*kairos*) to wash herself, using a normal Greek verb for washing or bathing. Getting into the water she says, "In the name of Jesus Anointed I cleanse myself on my last day." The Greek verb in this statement is *baptizomai*, normally transliterated, "I will baptize myself." There are two major problems with this transliteration. 1) By not translating *baptizomai*, the play on words between washing and cleansing is missed. 2) The transliteration "baptism" implies a Christian sacrament, a level of formalization inappropriate to the mid-second century. The ritual of cleansing was still evolving in this period, as is evident by Thecla's action. Despite Tertullian's scorn, other ancient authors discuss Thecla's action with no objection.[20] We should see this as one step on the road towards what would become the formal Christian sacrament of baptism by the end the second century. In support of this conclusion, Thecla cleanses herself in the name of Jesus Anointed without a baptismal formula. She does this because she thinks this is her last day.

The women interpret her act as suicide and even the governor is moved because of her beauty. The male gaze persists.

The lightning and cloud of fire are a divine epiphany that clearly manifests God's approval of what Thecla has done. God has taken her side all along. The lightning kills the seals and the cloud of smoke hides her nakedness.

Seals were common in the Mediterranean Sea and viewed as dangerous.

19. Synder, *Ante Pacem*, 38–41.
20. See Pervo, *The Acts of Paul*, 165.

10 (35) Upon more beasts being set upon Thecla, the women flood the arena with all manner of spices and aromatics that overwhelmed the wild beasts. This is like a game in which every offensive move is met with a blocking defense.

Alexander remains in charge. His status clearly trumps the governor's powers. But his newest proposal to execute Thecla once again goes astray and she escapes. His cash outlay is adding up and unless his wealth is immense, bankruptcy is not far away. The action is fast and focused. It also lacks realism. Arranging for such an elaborate series of games, wild beasts galore, and a water spectacle is unlikely for a single execution. Even more, the blocking of every move against Thecla begins to appear fantastic and even comic.

Tryphaena Is Dead 4.11–13

4.11 (36) *Tryphaena, while standing next to the railing near the arena, keeled over, so that her female slaves said, "Royal Tryphaena is dead." Therefore, the governor put a halt to the events, and all the city was scared. Then Alexander, falling at the governor's feet, said, "Have mercy on me and the city and set free the one condemned to the beasts, or else the city will be destroyed. For, if Caesar ever hears of these things, he will quickly destroy the city along with us, because his imperial relative Tryphaena died at the arena railing."*

12 (37) *Now the governor called Thecla out from the midst of the wild beasts and said to her, "Who are you? And what surrounds you so that none of the wild beasts touched you?"*

Then she said, "I am a slave of the living God. As to the things surrounding me, I have placed my trust in the one with whom God is well pleased, his son. Because of whom, not one of the wild beasts touched me. For he is the only mountain of salvation and the basis of life without death. For he is a refuge for the storm tossed, solace for the afflicted, shelter for the despairing, and in conclusion, whoever does not trust in him, will not live but die forever."

13 (38) *Upon hearing these things, the governor ordered clothing be brought in and said, "Put the clothes on." But she said, "The one who clothed my nakedness while I was fighting the wild beasts, this one will clothe me on the judgment day with salvation." And accepting the clothes, she put them on.*

Now immediately the governor issued a decree, saying, "I am releasing Thecla, the slave of God, the Godfearer, to you."

All the women cried out with a loud voice and as with a single voice gave praise to God saying, "One is god who has saved Thecla." The whole city was rocked with that voice.

Commentary

4.11 (36) The imagination strains to find other ways to try to kill Thecla. In the flurry, Tryphaena passes out, which brings the action to a complete standstill. Her slave women cry out, "Royal Tryphaena is dead." This announcement terrifies the city, the governor, and Alexander. They all fear imperial retribution. Alexander tries to quickly reverse what he has been vigorously pursuing. His plea to the governor is self-serving.

12 (37) The execution suddenly stops and the governor summons Thecla out from among the wild beasts. He does not resume questioning about her guilt but about her relation to the divine. He asks two questions. The first question, "Who are you?" inquires about her numinous status. The second question, "Who are you that you have such power?" asks about what powers are protecting her.

Thecla answers both questions. Her title is "a slave of God" (4.1, 6), a title she shares with Paul (3.4). God is specified as the living God, a Jewish title. The surrounding protecting power is God's son, "with whom God is well pleased," a clear reference to Jesus' baptism narrative in the synoptic gospels (Mark 1:11), which is appropriate following Thecla's own baptism. The images of rescue pile up, making a strong confession on Thecla's part. The concluding statement is a negative version of John 11:26: "everyone who lives and believes in me will never die."

13 (38) Thecla proclaims that God will clothe her on the judgment day, but she sensibly accepts the governor's offer of clothing. He issues an official decree releasing Thecla. *Acton*, decree, is a Latin loanword. He calls her slave of God, her preferred title, and a Godfearer, which would indicate that he sees her as aligned with Judaism.

The women who have consistently supported Thecla cry out with one voice so loudly that it rocks the city. "One is god" need not signify belief in the one God of Israel. It may mean that it is the god that got the job done.

The testing of the virgin is a major theme in romance novels. Thecla has come through her test with flying colors. This formally concludes Thecla's testing that Paul foretold in 3.25. Thecla did not fail, did not come close to failure as Paul had feared, and did receive the water with God's approval. God sanctioned her every move and approved her.

Tryphaena Lives 4.14

4.14 (**39**) *Now when the good news was announced to Tryphaena, she went with the crowd to meet Thecla and threw her arms around her and said, "Now I trust that the dead are raised. Now I trust that my child lives. Come inside, and everything that is mine I will sign over to you."*

Then Thecla went in with her and rested in her house for eight days, teaching her God's word, so that she trusted, as well as many of her female slaves. And the house was filled with great joy.

Commentary

4.14 (**39**) The narrative now picks up the loose ends to bring the whole cycle to a close, first with Tryphaena, then Paul (4.15–16), then Onesiphorus (4.17), and finally Thecla's mother (4.18).

After fainting away and appearing dead, Tryphaena's fate had dropped from view. Now the narrative returns to her story. "When the good news was announced" is a verb form commonly used in Paul's letters, the Gospel of Luke, and the Acts of the Apostles for proclaiming the good news (gospel). Here it appears to be used in a conventional sense, but it may have a double sense as it announces Thecla's being saved from death.

Tryphaena's confession goes to the heart of the gospel formula with which Paul's teaching was summarized in 3.1 and 3.5—resurrection, "my child lives." She takes Thecla into her house and signs over all her property, effectively adopting her as her daughter, implied all along but now made official. At the conclusion Thecla becomes a preacher of God's word. This is a household mission and the whole house is converted. Significantly, this is a house of females converted by a female, decidedly different from the picture of the same type of household conversions in the Acts of the Apostles.

Reunion with Paul 4.15–16

4.15 (**40**) *Thecla yearned for Paul and sought him and looked everywhere for him. And she was informed that he was in Myra. And taking young men and* women, she dressed up by stitching a woman's frock into a garment in the form of a man's clothing and departed for Myra. So, she found Paul speaking God's word and she went up to him. He was astounded at seeing her and the crowd with her, thinking that some other new test was upon her. Realizing this, she said to him, "I have been ritually bathed, Paul, for the one who worked with you for the good news has also worked with me for bathing."

16 (41) And taking her by the hand, Paul led her into the house of Hermias. And he listens to everything she had to report. Paul was totally amazed. And those who heard were invigorated and prayed for Tryphaena.

And Thecla, getting up, said to Paul, "I am going to Iconium." Paul said, "Go and teach God's word." Then Tryphaena sent her a large amount of clothing and gold to be distributed by Paul for the service of the poor.

Commentary

15 (40) The narrative turns to the next loose end, Paul. Thecla's yearning for Paul is her defining characteristic since the story's beginning when she sat at the window listening to Paul (3.7).

Myra is in southwest Turkey on the Mediterranean. It is mentioned in Acts 27:5–6. If Thecla is in Antioch of Pisidia it is a difficult journey of 242 miles (390 km). If in Antioch in Syria, it is a difficult sea voyage. The narrative is uninterested in geography, distance, or degree of difficulty. The journey simply happens.

Thecla travels with a group of young men and women. The note about men is odd. To this point, the narrative has shown no interest in men, except as villains, and no mention of men is made in connection with Tryphaena's household. The note about young men may be a later addition. But the narrative is interested in describing Thecla fashioning male looking clothes for the journey. No explanation is offered. Perhaps she is disguising herself for the dangers of the journey or perhaps she is experimenting with gender along the line of Galatians 3:26–28. In the *Passion of Andrew*, 20, Maximilla dresses as a man.[21]

Thecla's encounter with Paul parallels her last encounter in 3.25. There she had offered to cut off her hair like a man and to follow Paul. Paul resisted. Here she appears dressed as a man and Paul is astonished. In 3.25 Paul was afraid she would fail a future test, but now he thinks she is undergoing yet another test. Previously she had asked for the seal of water. Now

21. In MacDonald, *The Acts of Andrew*, 85.

she boldly states that she has been ritually bathed (baptized). Thecla draws an explicit comparison between what God has done for Paul and what God has done for her. They are effectively equals.

16 (41) The scene shifts to the house of Hermias. The APTh views all significant action among those who follow Jesus Anointed as taking place in houses. The public arena is a place of danger. In this light, praying for Tryphaena means praying for her house. Tryphaena's house/gathering/community then supports Paul's work among the poor. This mutual support played an important role in the Anointed's households.

Thecla's announcement that she is going to Iconium points back to the story's beginning. Homecoming of the lovers is standard in the romance novel. But in this case, the two lovers part. Even though most commentators see Paul's "Go and teach God's word," as Paul commissioning Thecla, that is not so clear. Since God has already commissioned Thecla, Paul's response is not her commissioning but a recognition and legitimization of what has already happened. It might also be seen as Paul's effort to bring Thecla under his control. If so, it fails, because she goes her own way.

The House of Onesiphorus 4.17–18

4.17 (42) *Then she departed for Iconium and entered the house of Onesiphorus and fell to the floor where Paul used to sit. She taught God's word and wept, saying, "O my God and the world's God, where the light has shown upon me, Anointed Jesus, son of God, my help in prison, my help before the governor, my help in the fire, my help with the wild beasts, he is God and to you is glory forever, Amen."*

18 (43) *And she found that Thamyris was dead, but her mother was alive. And calling to her mother she says to her, "Theokleia, my mother, are you able to trust that the Master lives in the skies? For if you are seeking wealth, the Master will give them to you through me. If you are seeking your child, look, I am standing next to you." And bearing witness to these things, she departed for Seleucia.*

Then after enlightening many by God's word, she fell asleep in a beautiful dream.

Commentary

17 (**42**) The return to Iconium has two parts: in the house of Onesiphorus and Thecla's mother. In returning home to Iconium, she goes first to the house of Onesiphorus where the story started. That household of the Anointed is her true home. Thecla finds the place where Paul used to sit and takes his place teaching God's word. Her teaching is a prayer of thanksgiving for God and the Anointed's protection of her in all her trials. In effect she replays the story.

    18 (**43**) Before the difficult confrontation with her mother, Thecla is informed (how?) that Thamyris is dead. The contrast is succinctly stated with no explanation. It is not clear where Thecla and her mother meet, but "calling" suggests at the house of Onesiphorus. She calls on her mother to turn to the Master because he will give her wealth, of what kind is not explained. Then she points to herself. "If you are seeking your child, look, I am standing next to you." There is no report as to Theokleia's response.

    Thecla departs for Seleucia where later a major shrine in her honor was constructed (see "Shrine" above). This story may serve as teleological legend legitimating Thecla's shrine in Seleuia. Endings are not a strong point in ancient storytelling and this one is no exception.

Further Readings

Barrier, Jeremy W. *The Acts of Paul and Thecla: A Critical Introduction and Commentary*. Wissenschaftliche Untersuchungen zum Neuen Testament 2/270. Tübingen: Mohr Siebeck, 2009.

This is Barrier's doctoral dissertation, and it reads as such. His research in establishing the Greek text and the versions in other ancient languages, especially Coptic, is excellent. Features a complete list of textual witnesses. His translation is wooden and static, and the commentary tends toward scholarly questions. His treatment of the Acts of Thecla in the context of the ancient romance novel is a noteworthy aspect of the book.

Pervo, Richard I. *The Acts of Paul: A New Translation with Introduction and Commentary*. Cascade Books, 2014.

Provides a modern but quirky translation of the extant parts of the Acts of Paul. Excellent critical comments on the Greek texts and the variants in other ancient languages. He attempts to work out how the author of the Acts of Paul integrated the Thecla story into the larger composition. With scholarly commentary and notes.

Kraemer, Ross Shepard. *Women's Religions in the Greco-Roman World: A Sourcebook*. New York: Oxford University Press, 2004. 299–308.

The title accurately describes what a reader will find in this excellent collection. If interested in women and religion in the ancient world, most writings, inscriptions, and textual evidence is here. The only thing missing is the artwork. Very helpful organization.

Bremmer, Jan N. "Bibliography of Thecla." In *Thecla: Paul's Disciple and Saint in the East and West.* Edited by J. W. Barrier, J. N. Bremmer, T. Nicklas, and A. Puig i Tàrrech, 379–85. Studies on Early Christian Apocrypha 12. Leuven: Peeters Publishers, 2017.

The most current bibliography.

Barrier, J. W., "The Acts of Paul and Thecla: the Historiographical Context." In *Thecla: Paul's Disciple and Saint in the East and West,* edited by J. W. Barrier, J. N. Bremmer, T. Nicklas, and A. Puig i Tàrrech, 327–50. Studies on Early Christian Apocrypha 12. Leuven: Peeters Publishers, 2017.

A summary of the various historical approaches to APTh.

MacDonald, Dennis R. *The Legend and the Apostle: The Battle for Paul in Story and Canon.* Westminster Press, 1983.

One of the first efforts to argue for oral stories behind the Acts of Paul and Thecla and to show how the Pastorals and the Acts of Paul and Thecla were contesting over the image of Paul. Still worth reading.

D'Angelo, Mary Rose, and Ross Shepard Kraemer, eds. *Women & Christian Origins.* New York: Oxford University Press, 1999.

A pioneering collection of wide-ranging essays by important feminist critics that examines how women were important influences in the beginnings of Christian communities.

Osiek, Carolyn, and Margaret Y. MacDonald, with Janet H. Tulloch. *A Woman's Place: House Churches in Earliest Christianity.* Minneapolis: Fortress, 2006.

House churches were the most important social location for early Christianity, and women were important in the household. An excellent examination of women's lives from an historical and feminist perspective.

Hylen, Susan. *A Modest Apostle: Thecla and the History of Women in the Early Church*. Oxford: Oxford University Press, 2015.

A recent study arguing for a more prominent role of women in leadership roles in the early church. She argues for less difference between the Pastorals and the Acts of Paul of Thecla than commonly recognized.

Bibliography

Barrier, Jeremy W. *The Acts of Paul and Thecla: A Critical Introduction and Commentary.* Wissenschaftliche Untersuchungen zum Neuen Testament 2/270. Tübingen: Mohr Siebeck, 2009.

———. "The Acts of Paul and Thecla: The Historiographical Context." In *Thecla: Paul's Disciple and Saint in the East and West*, edited by Jeremy W. Barrier et al., 327–50. Studies on Early Christian Apocrypha 12. Leuven: Peeters, 2017.

Barrier, Jeremy W., et al., eds. *Thecla: Paul's Disciple and Saint in the East and West.* Studies on Early Christian Apocrypha 12. Leuven: Peeters, 2017.

Batle, J. Amengual i. "The Cult of the Female Proto-Martyr and the Apostle Saint Thecla in Hispania." In *Thecla: Paul's Disciple and Saint in the East and West*, edited by Jeremy W. Barrier et al., 240–82. Studies on Early Christian Apocrypha 12. Leuven: Peeters, 2017.

Bauer, Walter. *Orthodoxy and Heresy in Earliest Christianity.* Edited by Robert A. Kraft. Philadelphia: Fortress, 1971.

Bollók, János. "The Description of Paul in the Acta Pauli." In *The Apocryphal Acts of Paul and Thecla*, edited by Jan N. Bremmer, 1–15. Studies on the Apocryphal Acts of the Apostles 2. Kampen: Kok Pharos, 1996.

Bremmer, Jan N. ed. *The Apocryphal Acts of Paul and Thecla.* Studies on the Apocryphal Acts of the Apostles 2. Kampen: Kok Pharos, 1996.

Brown, Peter. *The Body and Society: Men, Women and Sexual Renunciation in Early Christianity.* New York: Columbia University Press, 1988.

Brown, Raymond E. *An Introduction to the New Testament.* Anchor Bible Reference Library. New York: Doubleday, 1997.

Burrus, Virginia. *Chastity as Autonomy: Women in the Stories of the Apocryphal Acts.* Studies in Women and Religion 23. Lewiston, NY: Mellen, 1987.

Calef, Susan A. "Thecla 'Tried and True' and the Inversion of Romance." In *A Feminist Companion to the New Testament Apocrypha*, edited by Amy-Jill Levine and Maria Mayo Robbins, 163–85. London: T. & T. Clark, 2006.

Cardman, Francine. "Women, Ministry, and Church Order in Early Christianity." In *Women & Christian Origins*, edited by Mary Rose D'Angelo and Ross Shepard Kraemer, 300–329. New York: Oxford University Press, 1999.

Cooper, Kate. *The Virgin and the Bride: Idealized Womanhood in Late Antiquity.* Cambridge: Harvard University Press, 1999.

Curley, Michael J., trans. *Physiologus.* Austin: University of Texas Press, 1979.

D'Angelo, Mary Rose, and Ross Shepard Kraemer, eds. *Women & Christian Origins*. New York: Oxford University Press, 1999.

Davies, Stevan L. *The Revolt of the Widows: The Social World of the Apocryphal Acts*. Carbondale: Southern Illinois University Press, 1980.

Davis, Stephen J. "An Arabic Acts of Paul and Thecla: Text and translation, with Introduction and Critical Commentary." In *Thecla: Paul's Disciple and Saint in the East and West*. Edited by Jeremy W. Barrier et al., 105–51. Studies on Early Christian Apocrypha 12. Leuven: Peeters, 2017.

———. *The Cult of Saint Thecla: A Tradition of Women's Piety in Late Antiquity*. Oxford Early Christian Studies. Oxford: Oxford University Press, 2001.

Dewey, Arthur J., et al. *The Authentic Letters of Paul: A New Reading of Paul's Rhetoric and Meaning: The Scholars Version*. Salem, OR: Polebridge, 2010.

Dibelius, Martin, and Hans Conzelmann. *The Pastoral Epistles: A Commentary on the Pastoral Epistles*. Translated by Philip Buttolph and Adela Yarbro. Hermeneia. Philadelphia: Fortress, 1972.

Dulk, Matthijs den. "I Permit No Woman to Teach Except for Thecla, The Curious Case of the Pastoral Epistles and the *Acts of Paul* Reconsidered." *Novum Testamentum* 54 (2012) 176–203.

Ehrman, Bart D. "The Acts of Thecla." In *Lost Scriptures: Books That Did Not Make It into the New Testament*, 113–21. New York: Oxford University Press, 2003.

———. *A Brief Introduction to the New Testament*. 2nd ed. New York: Oxford University Press, 2009.

———. *Lost Christianities: The Battle for Scripture and the Faiths We Never Knew*. New York: Oxford University Press, 2003.

Elliott, J. K., ed. *The Apocryphal New Testament: A Collection of Apocryphal Christian Literature in an English Translation*. Oxford: Oxford University Press, 2005.

Galinsky, Karl. "Augustus' Legislation on Morals and Marriage." *Philologus* 125 (1981) 126–44.

Grubbs, Judith Evans. "Singles, Sex and Status in the Augustan Marriage Legislation." In *The Single Life in the Roman and Later Roman World*, edited by Sabine R. Huebner and Christian Laes, 105–24. Cambridge: Cambridge University Press, 2019.

Haines-Eitzen, Kim. *The Gendered Palimpsest: Women, Writing, and Representation in Early Christianity*. Oxford: Oxford University Press, 2012.

Harris, William V. *Ancient Literacy*. Cambridge: Harvard University Press, 1989.

Hennecke, Edgar, and Wilhelm Schneemelcher. *New Testament Apocrypha*, Vol. 2: *Writings Relating to the Apostles; Apocalypses and Related Subjects*. Philadelphia: Westminster, 1965.

Hylen, Susan E. *A Modest Apostle: Thecla and the History of Women in the Early Church*. Oxford: Oxford University Press, 2015.

Jacobs, Andrew. *The Life of Thecla: Apocryphal Expansion in Late Antiquity*. Westar Tools and Translations. Early Christian Apocrypha 11. Eugene, OR: Cascade Books, 2024.

———. *Life of St. Thecla (Ps.-Basil of Seleucia)*. http://andrewjacobs.org/translations/thecla.html.

James, M. R. *The Apocryphal New Testament, Being the Apocryphal Gospels, Acts, Epistles, and Apocalypses, with Other Narratives and Fragments*. Oxford: Clarendon, 1924.

Johnson, Scott Fitzgerald. *The Life and Miracles of Thekla: A Literary Study*. Hellenic Studies 13. Washington, DC: Center for Hellenic Studies, 2006.

Kraemer, Ross E. "Thecla of Iconium, Reconsidered." In *Unreliable Witnesses: Religion, Gender, and History in the Greco-Roman Mediterranean*, 117–52. Oxford: Oxford University, Press, 2011.

———. *Women's Religions in the Greco-Roman World: A Sourcebook*. New York: Oxford University Press, 2004.

Lefkowitz, Mary R., and Maureen B. Fant. *Women's Life in Greece and Rome: A Source Book in Translation*. 4th ed. Baltimore: Johns Hopkins University Press, 2016.

Levine, Amy-Jill, and Maria Mayo Robbins, eds. *A Feminist Companion to the New Testament Apocrypha*. Feminist Companion to the New Testament and Early Christian Writings 11. London: T. & T. Clark, 2006.

MacDonald, Dennis Ronald. *Acts of Andrew*. Early Christian Apocrypha 1. Santa Rosa, CA: Polebridge, 2005.

———. *The Legend and the Apostle: The Battle for Paul in Story and Canon*. Philadelphia: Westminster, 1983.

MacDonald, Dennis Ronald, and Andrew D. Scrimgeour. "Pseudo-Chrysostom's Panegyric to Thecla: The Heroine of the 'Acts of Paul' in Homily and Art." *Semeia* 38 (1986) 15–59.

McGinn, Sheila E. "The Acts of Thecla." In *Searching the Scriptures*, edited by Elisabeth Schüssler Fiorenza with Ann Brock and Shelly Matthews, 2:800–828. New York: Crossroad, 1993.

McGowan, Anne, and Paul F. Bradshaw. *The Pilgrimage of Egeria: A New Translation of the Itinerarium Egeriae with Introduction and Commentary*. Alcuin Club Collections 93. Collegeville, MN: Liturgical, 2018.

Misset-Van de Weg, Magda. "A Wealthy Woman Named Tryphaena: Patroness of Thecla of Iconium." In *The Apocryphal Acts of Paul and Thecla*, edited by Jan N. Bremmer, 16–35. Studies on the Apocryphal Acts of the Apostles 2. Kampen: Kok Pharos, 1996.

Morris, J. B, et al., trans. *The Homilies of St. John Chrysostom on the Epistle of St. Paul the Apostle to the Romans*. In A Select Library of the Nicene and Post-Nicene Fathers 11. Reprint, Grand Rapids: Eerdmans, 1979.

Osiek, Carolyn, and Margaret Y. MacDonald, with Janet H. Tulloch. *A Woman's Place: House Churches in Earliest Christianity*. Minneapolis: Fortress, 2006.

Perkins, Judith, *The Suffering Self: Pain and Narrative Representation in the Early Christian Era*. London: Routledge, 1995.

Pervo, Richard I. *The Acts of Paul: A New Translation with Introduction and Commentary*. Eugene, OR: Cascade Books, 2014.

———. *Dating Acts: Between the Evangelists and the Apologists*. Santa Rosa, CA: Polebridge, 2006.

———. *The Pastorals and Polycarp: Titus, 1–2 Timothy, and Polycarp to the Philippians*. Scholars Bible. Salem, OR: Polebridge, 2016.

Roberts, Alexander, et al., eds. *The Ante-Nicene Fathers: Translations of the Writings of the Fathers down to A.D. 325*. American reprint of the Edinburgh edition. New York: Scribner, 1925.

Scott, Bernard Brandon. *The Real Paul: Recovering His Radical Challenge*. Salem, OR: Polebridge, 2015.

Smith, Dennis E., and Joseph B. Tyson, eds. *Acts and Christian Beginnings: The Acts Seminar Report*. Salem, OR: Polebridge, 2013.

Snyder, Graydon F. *Ante Pacem: Archaeological Evidence of Church Life before Constantine*. Macon, GA: Mercer University Press, 2003.

Streete, Gail C. "Buying the Stairway to Heaven: Perpetua and Thecla as Early Christian Heroines." In *A Feminist Companion to the New Testament Apocrypha*, edited by Amy-Jill Levine and Maria Mayo Robbins, 186–205. Feminist Companion to the New Testament and Early Christian Writings 11. London: T. & T. Clark, 2006.

———. *Redeemed Bodies: Women Martyrs in Early Christianity*. Louisville: Westminster John Knox, 2009.

Tertullian. "On Baptism." In *The Ante-Nicene Fathers: Translations of the Writings of the Fathers down to A.D. 325*, edited by Alexander Roberts et al., 3:669–80. American reprint of the Edinburgh edition. New York: Scribner, 1925.

Vander Stichele, Caroline, and Todd C. Penner. *Contextualizing Gender in Early Christian Discourse: Thinking Beyond Thecla*. London: T. & T. Clark, 2009.

Vearncombe, Erin, et al. *After Jesus before Christianity: A Historical Exploration of the First Two Centuries of Jesus Movements*. New York: HarperOne, 2021.

Voicu, Sever J. "Thecla in the Christian East." In *Thecla: Paul's Disciple and Saint in the East and West*, edited by Jeremy W. Barrier et al., 47–68. Studies on Early Christian Apocrypha 12. Leuven: Peeters, 2017.

www.ingramcontent.com/pod-product-compliance
Lightning Source LLC
Chambersburg PA
CBHW031147090426
42738CB00008B/1249